MINISTERING
TO THE
GRIEF SUFFERER

SUCCESSFUL PASTORAL COUNSELING SERIES

MINISTERING TO THE GRIEF SUFFERER

C. CHARLES BACHMANN, Ph.D.

PRENTICE-HALL, INC., ENGLEWOOD CLIFFS, N.J.

Ministering to the Grief Sufferer
by C. Charles Bachmann, Ph.D.

Library of Congress Catalog Card Number: 64–14539

Printed in the United States of America

T 58430

Second printing . . . . December, 1965

PRENTICE-HALL INTERNATIONAL, INC., *London*
PRENTICE-HALL OF AUSTRALIA, PTY., LTD., *Sydney*
PRENTICE-HALL OF CANADA, LTD., *Toronto*
PRENTICE-HALL OF INDIA (PRIVATE) LTD., *New Delhi*
PRENTICE-HALL OF JAPAN, INC., *Tokyo*

To my wife, Mary Lee,
and my children, Rhonda Lu and Charles McKay,
who had the patience to bear with me
while "Daddy wrote his book."

ACKNOWLEDGMENTS

Chaucer once said: "Gladly would he learn . . . gladly teach." When one has been taught by others, he has the obligation and opportunity to pass on a legacy of learning to those who follow. Without the help of others no endeavor is attempted. Without God's help many things would have been left undone. I gratefully acknowledge my teachers past and present and all who have made this volume possible, especially my counselees, pastor and funeral director friends who were so cooperative in this venture. In addition my appreciation is expressed to: the General Editor, Russell L. Dicks who felt that there was something helpful I could say and to my wife who patiently labored over phrases with me till it was said, and my secretary Beverly Ruttinger who typed and retyped what needed to be said.

INTRODUCTION

This series of books represents the most comprehensive publishing effort ever made in the field of pastoral care. These books could not have been published twenty-five years ago or probably even ten, for the material was not then available. In the past, single books have been available covering different phases of the task. Now we are bringing the subjects together in a single series. Here we present a library of pastoral care covering the major topics and problems that most pastors will encounter in their ministry. Fortunately, not all of these problems need be faced every week or even every month. But, when they are, the minister wants help and he wants it immediately.

These books are prepared for the nonspecialized minister serving the local church, where he is the most accessible professional person in the community. It is a well-accepted fact that more people turn to clergy when in trouble than to all other professional people. Therefore, the pastor must not fail them.

Russell L. Dicks
General Editor

PREFACE

It is almost ten years since the appearance of Dr. Erich Lindemann's classic article: "Symptomatology and Management of Acute
Grief." Dr. Lindemann is Psychiatrist-in-Chief, Massachusetts General Hospital and Professor of Psychiatry, Harvard Medical School.
The article was occasioned by his pioneer work with the survivors
and families of the victims who perished in the Cocoanut Grove
holocaust. He pointed out the necessity of doing normal "grief work."
He stated what others, who have followed have reiterated, that it is
necessary for the grief sufferer to work through the loss step-by-step
until the sufferer is free from the "bondage to the deceased" and can
lead an independent life with the "image of the deceased" i.e. being
able to live with the memories and the hurts, the joys and sorrows.
No one, he affirmed, escapes this process of grief work or is ever free
until he does work through the grief.

This thesis has been repeated by others like his co-worker Dr.
Clemens Benda, also a psychiatrist of Massachusetts General and
Harvard Medical School. His article: "Bereavement and Grief Work"
first delivered at the Buffalo Pilot Project in 1961 (a joint meeting
of clergy and funeral directors) re-emphasized the salient points made
by Lindemann but stressed that clergymen and funeral directors need
to work closely together. Lindemann had suggested this in 1960
when he addressed the National Funeral Directors Convention in
Denver. He said clergy are a part of the "care taking" groups. They
are on the front line of this experience.

Works by clergymen, like William Rogers who wrote his doctoral
dissertation on "The Place of Grief Work in Mental Health," (Boston University, 1949), and subsequently published *Ye Shall Be
Comforted*, (Philadelphia, Westminster Press, 1950); Paul Irion,

The Funeral and the Mourners, (New York, Abingdon Press, 1954), which stresses the individual nature of the funeral; Edgar Jackson, *Understanding Grief,* (New York, Abingdon Press, 1957), which attempts to explore the underlying philosophy in the grief process, and Granger Westberg's monograph, *Good Grief,* (Rock Island, Ill., Augustana Press, 1962), a sermon originally delivered at Rockefeller Chapel, University of Chicago, to be used by the grief sufferer in understanding his grief, all attest to the growing interest in the subject among the clergy.

There is also an ever increasing awareness on the part of funeral directors of the important aspects of bereavement beyond the providing of essential burial services. The whole funeral field seems to be under attack, at this moment, with the recent printing of the books by Ruth Mulvey Harmer, *The High Cost of Dying,* (New York, Crowell-Collier Press, 1963) and Jessica Mitford, *The American Way of Death,* (New York, Simon & Schuster, Inc., 1963). These books deal mainly with an attack upon the funeral directing field and tend to be on the side of sensationalism, concentrating mostly on costs and caskets and cremations or quick disposals.

There is another side of the question which has to be faced by the pastor in his work-a-day world, i.e., how will he minister to the grief sufferer? This is the concern of the present volume.

The pastor, of all helping specialists, stands in a unique relationship to the grief sufferer, because he is the one person in the community to whom families continually turn for some form of pastoral care. This is most clearly demonstrated at the time of death, though grief is experienced in other crises situations which result in severing the ties of relationship—divorce, separation, loss of job, amputations, and illnesses to mention just a few.

It would be unthinkable to conduct a burial service without a clergyman, priest or rabbi officiating. Yet the pastor has not always fully been aware of the role he must play in relationship to the grief sufferer. This is one of the roles, however, he cannot "shove aside" nor turn over to others. He needs to be more sure of himself, in his ministry to the grief sufferer and to assume the pastoral role of *seelsorge*—the care of and cure of souls—with a kind of understanding and helpfulness, which no one else can provide.

This volume is designed to offer some encouragement and some practical helps to assist the pastor to make the most of the opportunities he has to help the grief sufferers in one of the most critical times of their existence. He is thus privileged, "to walk in the company of the hurt."

CONTENTS

CHAPTER ONE

The MEANING Of GRIEF

Grief is an emotion. It involves the feeling life of a person. It is a tearing kind of emotion, because it shuts off the person from fulfillment of hope, dreams, and aspirations. Its frustration is felt deeply inside the being—hard to reach, define, or explain to anyone else. It is psychic pain; it hurts. It is deeply embedded in the feeling life, sometimes inaccessible. Like love, hate, and fear—the three primary emotions—grief is bound closely in a kinship, and at times embraces all three. In the immediate loss, the sufferer may experience all these emotions as he recounts and remembers previous occasions when these feelings reigned. The memories remain, but the loss adds frustration and pain. Grief can be expressed, repressed or suppressed, for these are ways of dealing with emotions.

Grief is a normal emotion, although sometimes it appears to the onlooker that the grief sufferer is not acting normally. Others will often try to short-circuit this expression of grief, believing that the bereaved is "carrying on," and they will try to divert attention to more pleasant aspects of the former relationship or to some wholly inconsequential activity. This means that the friend, relative, or whoever it may be is reacting to his own attitude toward death or the person, or to his own discomfiture in trying to be of help to the grief sufferer. This tendency to cover up or cover over or channelize the thinking of the bereaved seldom meets with success because it tends to deny outlet to a perfectly normal emotional response.

The grieving person, sometimes acceding to the cultural demands, the mores of the group, or community expectation, may tend to delay or even deny his or her reaction or to observe the death in an unrealistic way—not giving in to emotion because it may be misinterpreted as not exemplifying the confidence of the Christian, "that

nothing can separate. . . ." In reality it is tearing him to pieces. He
will not let go because someone might think him unchristian or not
manifesting faith in Christ. This is grossly misleading because it
seems to suggest that expressing the emotion of grief is denied to the
Christian, or that somehow he, being more than human, is supposed
to rise above this transitory existence. He is human and vulnerable
and subject to emotions just as any other of God's creatures. It would
be just as pointless to say that a Christian should not express love or
fear or hate, that somehow he is immune *to* or *from* emotions.

There is no denial in the witness of a Christian because the sufferer is capable of expressing emotion. There has been a current mis-
conception of denying expression because we have been conditioned
by a kind of stoicism that says one must bear up bravely because
other members of the "communion of saints" are watching to see how
suffering is going to be borne. It would appear that because one is a
Christian he can go through the experience of great loss automati-
cally and somehow come smiling through, exuding confidence. One
is not so sure that Christians are any more immune to emotion than
the rest of the community. They may have a certain number of resources, which can be utilized at the time of the bereavement; they
are not spared, however, going through the process of grief and working through the loss from the first pangs of despair to eventual release from "the bondage to the deceased."[1] Dr. Erich Lindemann,
Chief of Psychiatry at Massachusetts General Hospital, Boston, Massachusetts, early called attention to the process of grief work and the
psychological necessity for the person experiencing loss to demon-
strate eventually that he is free to be himself again. This is especially
true if the relationship was very close and a strong bond of mutual
dependency existed. Only those whose sensitivities are blunted by unhappy remembrances will have a hard time working through the accompanying feelings. The first shock waves of this emotional flood can
almost completely inundate the most determined kind of resistance to
the acceptance of loss. Its engulfing finality sounds many unresolved
chords.

[1] Erich Lindemann, "Symptomatology and Management of Acute Grief,"
American Journal of Psychiatry, 101 (September 1944), 141. Reprinted in
Journal of Pastoral Care, 5 (Fall 1951), 19–31.
This classic article was occasioned by treatment of the survivors and relatives
of the tragic Cocoanut Grove Fire in Boston in 1942.

This leads naturally to a discussion of what may be expected in the loss of a loved one or a not-so-loved one. There are certain physical as well as psychological reactions that may be expected. If a person does not experience all or even some of them, it does not mean that he has not reacted properly. These reactions are *more* or *less*—a question of degree and intensity. This can be illustrated by a story told to me by a friend who frequently vacations in Mexico. He said that the first time he went to the doctor he was given the usual inoculations, but the physician didn't tell him what reaction to expect from the shots. If he had just said: "You'll likely feel achy, uncomfortable for a day or so; you could even run a high temperature," the patient would not have been so unprepared for the reaction that followed his inoculations. In much the same way, if a person knows something of the grief reaction pattern, he is not so likely to be thrown by the situation.

Physical Reactions

When you ask a person who has just experienced a loss what his reaction is, he may be speechless as if struck by a thunderbolt. This is especially true if he does not see the person die or if the onset of illness is sudden and climactic or if there is an accident involved. There is often physical reaction like a sudden desire to throw oneself into a heap, to faint away, or to stand as if transfixed. If a person has died in the hospital and the message is given over the phone, the relative or close friend may drop the receiver and even experience sharp pain and loss of consciousness. This is often the reason why hospital personnel say when calling next of kin in the event of death: "Mr. Smith has taken a turn for the worse," when the person, in actuality, has died. They wait until the doctor who took care of the patient can meet and relate the message. At the hospital there are persons available to handle the first waves of immediate reaction. One has seen the highly emotionalized response of running aimlessly down the corridor toward the room or ward where the patient had died, screaming all the way, having to be restrained by hospital personnel.

The initial shock is frequently followed by such physical symptoms as: queasiness in the stomach, sharp pain in the abdomen, pounding or throbbing in the head, the cottony feeling in the mouth, the loss of awareness of surroundings, and palpitation of the heart. Since a great many people die in hospitals, this becomes increasingly the burden of the medical profession and those who work closely in the team relationship. Who tells the survivors and how they are told make a great deal of difference. After the initial shock wave it is important to have people who understand near by. This is why the pastor-chaplain is present at times of crises such as death. This has always been true in the military. Many times the military chaplain has had the responsibility of notifying the next of kin, because it was felt that he was able to be supportive to the bereaved after the initial shock.

During the bereavement, these physical manifestations may become more pronounced and continue for days or weeks. The period of mourning is characterized by a state of unreality as that of the person who when "knocked off his pins" attempts to fight for and gain equilibrium. Other physical manifestations experienced by the grief sufferer are: sighing, feeling empty, and loss of appetite. The fog of unreality is the most common characteristic. This is especially true if the individual has been hardy and robust and full of fun and life and a few hours or days later suddenly succumbs. One hears: "I just can't believe Joe is dead; why I was taking to him on the phone only a few days ago. He seemed so jolly and quick-witted." This is illustrated by the story of a pastor in a large Midwestern parish which had been built largely by his dynamic efforts, whose life was suddenly snuffed out by a group of irresponsible teen-agers playing Russian roulette with an automobile. Each day on the way to school they would drive from a blind country road, their vision blocked by large corn fields on both sides of the road, into the main United States highway. It happened once too often and they rammed the pastor's car, killing him instantaneously. The widow, injured in the accident, was unable to go to the funeral and a year later still walked as if in a trance.

For some, death is an incalculable loss that somehow the grief sufferer does not want to believe. He keeps going over and over the story raising ultimate questions: "How can this be?" "Why did it happen?" "Why did God allow this to happen?" "How will I ever be able to get on without him/her?" In the family unit, the corporation, the organization, the Church, or wherever the individual impact of this person's life was great, a large gap is left that seemingly cannot be filled.

The acute grief and shock, the stunned nature of reaction is of sudden onset and felt immediately as if one were suddenly smitten. Some people may require days, weeks, or months before the full realization is apparent and accepted. This happened to a family, known to the writer, whose son was struck and killed by a car. The parents still have the feeling that their little son is going to come bursting through the door at any moment.

Psychological Factors

Paralleling—often accompanying and closely related to—the physical reactions are the emotional reactions to stress, which produce change in normal habitual patterns. Any kind of emotional distress can produce psychological change. Highly agitated patterns of behavior, an increase in activity of a highly random nature, talkativeness, and a lack of meaning in the routine affairs of normal day-to-day activity are observed.

It is normal for the grief sufferer to want to talk about the deceased, even to the extent of "idealizing," covering over the faults, denying that the relationship was anything but idyllic. The idea that the marriage was far from perfect is temporarily abandoned. There is often the rehearsal of the last days and hours, which presents an opportunity for the pastor to begin to take an active role in counseling, especially employing the ministry of listening to the bereaved as they rehearse over and over again the closing events, the last words, cherishing each moment as it is relived. Where one is allowed to ventilate, to tell the story in great detail, there is release of feeling and the beginning of the acceptance of the pain of loss. It becomes the sharing of the burden with someone who will listen with "the third ear"—the inner ear—to what is going on in the grief process.

Since grief is an emotion, it finds expression or it will be denied and/or delayed, to find an expression at a later day when the stimulus which produced the reaction does not seem to be related at all. Tears are the most common outer expression for intense feeling of deep emotion. We have tear ducts for this reason. God gave them for the purpose of expressing sorrow or loss. The late Rabbi Joshua L.

Leibman in his best seller *Peace Of Mind*[2] devoted a chapter to "Grief's Slow Wisdom" to elaborate this idea. We should not be ashamed to show tears, nor should we deny that we have these deep feelings that produce this kind of emotion. Many preachers have been embarrassed by the tears, and consider the funeral service a total failure because they were not able to preach so that people retain their composure. This simply discourages the expression and may cause the bereaved to avoid grieving ever. You have heard it said as I have: "I never shed a tear." This person may be more deeply in trouble than someone who has allowed full, normal expression of feeling. Full expression will never cause a person mental illness. It is, again, a curious part of our cultural heritage here in America that we put a premium on the stoic concealment of emotional reaction patterns. Giving vent to feeling through tears or verbal expression is the best mental health insurance. A general and genuine fear of the grief sufferer is that he will become mentally ill and suffer a nervous breakdown. He fears that this will be the consequence if he gives way to grief. Precisely the opposite is true.

Though no accurate statistics are available, it has been estimated that about 10 percent of the admissions to mental hospitals are persons suffering from unresolved grief problems related to bereavement. Adding to this the many other kinds of grief reactions caused by separation, rejection, divorce, etc., this percentage estimate should probably be much higher. Psychiatrists and pastor-chaplains who work in mental hospitals report that it would surprise the average citizen and the local parish pastor how many such people there are.

On the other hand, there are some who can express no emotion, who show distorted reactions, which is a defense in order not to lose control. This denial of real feeling reaches its zenith with those who enter into the fantasy that the deceased is not really dead but has gone away for a short time. The Christian faith sometimes gives illusory evidence to this phenomenon, because it is always seen in the context of a future that is not now. What we are saying has to do with the denial, sometimes the disguised fantasy that the deceased is only asleep. Compulsive rituals may be employed in an effort to preserve the illusion. These rituals may take the form of setting the table with an empty plate, laying out the person's clothes, keeping the room

---

[2] New York: Simon & Schuster, Inc., 1946.

exactly as it was before death, talking to the pictures of the deceased, visiting the cemetery, or engaging in some kind of psychic communion with the dead.[3]

The Buffalo Evening News, in 1961, carried the story of a woman, now in the State Hospital, who secreted the body of her mother between mattresses and applied various potions and oils to preserve the body. The bizarre feature of this story was that she had done this for a period of fifteen years. When one saw the almost perfectly preserved mummy it could not be denied that some people may go to great lengths to avert the reality of loss.

Guilt and hostility are common factors. One of the psychological manifestations either observed or in many cases suppressed or repressed, in addition to the extremely morbid reaction, is that many grief reactions find expression in other common phenomena such as guilt and hostility. Guilt, or more correctly, guilt feeling is usually expressed not so much in action as in words. "I should have gotten mother to the doctor sooner; if I had gotten Dr. so-and-so, things would have been different." These are guilt feelings because real guilt is felt only when there is actually a connection between the event and the person's relationship to it. This may also be seen when the person lives at a distance and the relative, friend, or parent suddenly dies and he is unable to get there prior to the moment of death. The feeling is that if he had been there in time Mother would have known and he would feel more comforted or his presence would have had some meaning. No doubt it would, but one does not have to castigate or in other ways flagellate oneself because he didn't get to the dying person's bedside in time. Guilt feelings may also be occasioned by remembrances of an argument or altercation with the deceased when time ran out before amends could be made or the interpersonal relationship improved or repaired. Here, again, the pastor who knows his parishioners can be aware of the dynamics of this relationship and prepare himself to minister in such a way that the bereaved feels he is understood and that he can experience cleansing by confessing such a fault or feeling. This is accomplished

---

[3] It was most notably recounted in Catherine Marshall's provocative To Live Again (New York: McGraw-Hill, Inc., 1957) that she tried this kind of communication before she accepted the reality of Peter Marshall's death.

not by faulty reassurance, which never reassures anyway, but by simple statement of support. The pastor might honestly affirm: "From my observation, everybody did what he could." This is a form of creative assertion; there is no need to reinforce the guilt or to make the guilty feel guiltier.

Reaction to guilt sometimes finds its expression in overspending on funeral arrangements, buying a more expensive casket or tombstone, or giving more to philanthropic organizations and various causes as a "peace offering" to atone for the guilty conscience for what was not done. If this is done, however, it may be worth the price and should not be unnecessarily condemned. It may save countless medical-psychiatric bills later, so long as it does not deplete the family resources in the process.

Hostility. Hostile feelings are another common manifestation. These are sometimes directed at the doctor who took care of the individual, or the nurse, funeral director, pastor or whoever may be closest at hand when the full force of the blow strikes. It is usually a senseless striking back to get rid of the feeling. It is a displaced feeling and is usually meant for the deceased. It seems as if the grief sufferer is saying: "Why did he have to die and leave me all alone to raise these children? I have to go out now and get a job. I will have to get along on less." It is like an angry fist raised against the sky. Because she cannot openly take out this resentment against God she may heap this abuse upon the unsuspecting pastor. He has to be aware that it isn't meant for him. There is a chance, however, that if the pastor has been too direct in his course of action prior to the death of the deceased he may get the full force broadside, and it really may be meant for him. This should teach him to be a bit wary about handing out advice too readily without deliberating over a longer period of time. Such reaction patterns are often seen where the minister has had a part in the hospitalization, or has taken the person to the hospital and stood by while surgery was performed.

It is well to recognize that these feelings of guilt and hostility can be mobilized in the counseling relationship. This will have to be after the funeral. If the pastor has done his pre-funeral work well, there may be opportunity to get into these matters later when the person can sit down and sort out these feelings in a less charged atmosphere. Here is a rare opportunity for the pastor to make the most of his skills in helping a person express these negative feelings in a controlled atmosphere. Here the individual can begin to face up to the loss, entertain the ambivalent feelings of idealization and hostility about the same person. In this way the grief sufferer will know that he is understood and accepted. This communicates that one may still be in a state of grace even though he may entertain hostile thoughts.

Grief's ambivalent character. Part of the ambivalent character of the grief syndrome is the entertaining of both negative and positive feelings about the person both before and after death. These are strong pulls of great intensity—the fist shaken at the sky and the most tender feeling aroused about the same individual in the same thought sequence and possibly in the same sentence. "Why did you have to die and leave me?" and tenderly, "Oh, George, how can I ever go on to face life without you?" Guilt and hostility feelings are a part of the psychological arsenal that the grief sufferer may carry around for a long time and fail to discharge because he may be afraid to face the facts of his existence. If he does express these feelings he needs to know that he may be reacting within the limits of that illusive goal—normalcy!

Part of the pastor's task is to detect the booby traps, and safely defuse them before they detonate. He can do this by patient, painstaking coverage of the territory which the grief sufferer must travel. He will have to know that individuals most often react to grief crises as they have reacted to other crises. He will also be prepared for the fact that the assigned role is not the one that is always played. He will have to be willing to ride with the grief sufferer over some rough roads. This may consume some important hours when he could be doing something else in the parish, more noticeable to the rest of the flock. There is no finer task than to have helped an individual to the place where the sufferer can say: "Thanks a lot pastor for listening; I can go it alone from here."

Grief seen as crisis. Many of life's crisis situations can be thought of as grief reactions. Grief is usually thought of as reaction to the loss of a loved one, but it can be reaction to loss of some more or less intangible things such as love, or a loved object, and/or material possessions. When one has invested a great deal of self in the life of another and the person leaves, walks out of one's life, agrees to a separation, or accepts a divorce settlement, some of the same physiological and psychological reactions are experienced. The grief syndrome can be extended to one who loses a job, position, power, or prestige, or to patients in hospitals who have to face life with the loss of limbs. Even those who have experienced removal of an internal organ often speak of this loss in terms of being less than a whole person. There is a profound sense of shock. They have been bereft! Here the grief is turned in upon oneself in a most dramatic way. This is true, especially, if the loss was occasioned by an accident and the incapacitation was necessitated because one had been careless or intoxicated. The remorse may be just as profound. It is removing of oneself from the community because of resulting incapacity.

Grief as separation. The separation phenomenon approximates the grief syndrome in marked ways, especially in a younger person. This, however, may not be on the conscious level. For example, children in a children's home have a similar kind of grief reaction when separated from parental homes as a result of separation or divorce. In such a home environment, one characteristic predominates, that is, the hope to return to the family circle. Where the separation persists as a result of divorce the adjustment may be made in superficial fashion, but the child may carry the emotional residue into adult life and it may not be resolved in his own marital relationships. Children here have difficulty also in relating to the parent figure who left the family circle. It represents a break in an important relationship, hence, grief. If it occurs in the early formative years, it has a marked effect. It may erupt in highly charged emotional situations, especially around the holidays. The deprivation that is felt at these particular moments is as profound as loss by death. Not only does this represent a break in an important relationship but it is thought of as rejection. Usually because the court awards the child to the mother, the feelings of rejection may be felt toward the father. This is often compounded in adoptions where one sees this acted out because of rejection by the original parent, even though the child may be adopted into a particularly congenial home atmosphere.

There seems to be an endless search for identity, a searching for the parents and a gnawing, aching which we have described as grief.

Grief as a disease entity. Grief has not often been thought of as a disease entity, but some psychiatrists are beginning to discover that significant losses have definite etiological factors, with a predictable course, degrees of disability, and a prognosis of recovery or failure to recover. These are comparable to other stress factors in living, which are just as real and intense, producing *pneumo-psycho-somatic (spiritual-mental-physical)* changes. Often the course of treatment in medical problems is influenced more by how the person reacts to stress situations than by any organic process. A man may have had no physical problems until he begins to go downhill financially. Business failures may have been glossed over to the extent that the issues of life just became too burdensome. These losses, while financial, were covered over and ignored and, therefore, never fully accepted or resolved. As in the grief process, recovery takes place when the wound heals. The residual psychic scar is a reminder that loss has occurred. While the body may accommodate the wound, its effect remains. Whether one successfully assimilates the loss into his experience depends on acceptance of the fact of loss.

Anticipatory grief. Grief may also be said to have an anticipatory character. Dr. Erich Lindemann first called attention to this characteristic of the grief reaction. He noted, quite accurately, this phenomenon in the relatives of the survivors of the Cocoanut Grove disaster. Many relatives anticipated the death of their loved ones in the disaster and then had to deal with the fact of their "return from the dead." It is akin to the departure of a soldier or sailor for overseas duty during wartime. The family anticipated so greatly that he would be killed that they went through the formal grief process in anticipation of the fact that he would not return. Often when he did return, the unrealness of the situation and the fantasy, in fact, of living with a phantom were encountered.

This phenomenon can be observed also in the hospital situation when a patient lingers for a long period. The relatives may anticipate so much the death of a father or mother, for example, that, in their minds, they already buried him or her before he actually dies. They go through the usual grief process before death, and observers may report a tearless grief reaction.

Dr. Lindemann has said: "Grieving and mourning is a skilled process, some people are lucky to discover it, some people have wise friends who happen to give them a hint, some people can't discover it, or can't do it because it is too painful. . . . These are some people whom we should discover early."[4]

The essential task for the pastor is sharing of the person's grief, allowing the person to become free from the bondage to the deceased, and finding new patterns of interpersonal relationship. The closer the relationship, the deeper the attachment to the deceased, the more important it is to provide proper atmosphere for formal grief work. An adequate therapy for bereavement acknowledges that there are two essentials for the sufferer in the grief process: (1) to relive and be relieved and to be able to assimilate the experience; (2) to be able to live with memories, the hurts and the suffering, the joys and the happiness in more or less comfortable fashion.

It is important for the pastor to realize that people's emotions are real and ought not to be covered up. It is essential for the pastor: (1) to recognize that a person who is experiencing grief may not be acting in keeping with his usual approach to life's situations; (2) to remember that when a person's life has been closely tied to another there is bound to be pain of loss and this cannot be denied outlet without its erupting later in something more serious; (3) to recall that the Church's responsibility is not to teach people to bear up stoically to great loss, especially the loss of loved ones or not-so-loved ones; (4) to reassess the teaching regarding the tendency to equate strong grief reaction with lack of faith, which allows for no expression of feeling; (5) to reopen the issues of life and death with the grief sufferer so that he can properly mourn, and (6) to encourage the mourner to build new bridges of relationship, both human and Divine.

---

[4] Erich Lindemann, "Psychological Aspects of Mourning," *The Director*, January 1961, 14–17. An address delivered at National Funeral Directors Association Meeting, Denver, Colorado, 1960.

CHAPTER TWO

The PASTOR'S RELATIONSHIP
To The GRIEF SUFFERER

No one really escapes coming to grips with the loss of loved ones through death or the loss experienced in other forms of crises, such as rejection, separation, etc. No family's life is spared this reality; it has a universal character.

The pastor, of all the helping specialists, stands in a unique relationship to the grief sufferer. He still has uninvited access and entrée to the homes of his parishioners and is expected to call. His handling of grief situations can prove decisive in the recovery of equilibrium and the return of the sufferer to pneumo-psycho-somatic balance. There is a natural inclination to turn to the pastor in crises.[1]

The image of the pastor is one that exemplifies, among other symbolizations, the spirit of Him who came to comfort and to heal broken relationships. This has been the pastor's peculiar responsibility because the Church has something specific to say about death. The relationship he has had with the grief sufferer determines how much help he can bring in time of grief crises. If the pastor has a real sensitivity to the needs of others he will be, or will become, aware of how his presence or person may be utilized to the best advantage. Usually because he can be more objective than relatives or other friends, the pastor can communicate the concern of the God whom he serves, the Church he represents, and the community in which he works. He can, by his presence, symbolize that profound hope which is not always verbalized—that God does not forsake His children in the most critical periods of their existence.

---

[1] Gerald Gurin, Joseph Veroff and Sheila Feld, *Americans View Their Mental Health* (New York: Basic Books Inc., 1960).

In times of grief the pastor's own personality, feelings, or attitudes toward death, grief, and the grief sufferer will either handicap or enhance his ability to be a part of the helping process. The role of the pastor in the therapy for bereavement will be proportionate to his relationship previously established, prior to death and grief, and how meaningful this relationship was. The pastor must be aware that the real needs may come after the ceremony is over, when the person or persons fight for recovery of balance and new patterns of relationship, and when all the ambivalences have to be faced.

The mystery which surrounds death and the pastor's own reactions shrouds death with the feeling of helplessness and even at times hopelessness. There has been confusion about the fact of death and the theological concept: "There is no death!" This aspect of existence, therefore, is often treated by exhortation rather than by exploration.

The pastor needs to know himself, operationally, before he is in a position to help others. This is the task of honestly facing up to himself, knowing his own strengths and weaknesses, the boundaries and limitations of his own resources, knowing what are his own basic anxieties, dependencies, and hostilities. "Knowing one's self," as the ancient Greeks said, is essential to any kind of relationship or to anyone in a helping relationship. This requires the "look see" into the hidden recesses of the self. It means self-study, self-appraisal, self-analysis, and self-understanding. Much could be said under each of these headings. Self-understanding is necessary for both professional and psychological survival.

The pastor cannot minister to people in any crisis situation if he is in ill health or if he himself is a psychological cripple. One can only minister to crisis or grief out of a reasonable degree of health and if he is among those in the community most sound in body, mind, and spirit.

In the local parochial situation the pastor is exposed to the grief crisis on a daily basis. Hardly a week goes by that he is not asked to officiate at a funeral. This demands stability. He is not always prepared for the way his parishioners might act or react. He may be able to take minor blows with some resilience, but to see a grief stricken person extremely upset, in uncontrollable agony at the death of those in close relationship, may shake his composure.

The pastor has to live closely with people to know them; he must live at close range with himself. Because one is a pastor does not exempt him either from feelings or from illness. This demands an elastic concept of self and health. It means that he must cultivate the capacity to accept limitations. It may also be translated to mean knowing what persons can be helped, or that "being all things to all men" is not always possible or permissible. One may work very intensely with a relatively few people, so the pastor should not feel guilty if he cannot work with everyone or work as well with one as with another. He needs to look critically at himself because the more he is aware of himself the fewer defenses he will raise.

The pastor probably cannot afford analysis in the sense of paid professional psychiatry, but he can practice self-analysis in the sense of digging into his guarded and staked-off areas to see if there are things which he ought to get rid of in order to be freer to help others. He may discover, if he is completely honest with himself, that he has some blind spots. If he is not able to undertake this kind of self-examination or if it leads only to circular thinking, then perhaps he needs to talk things over with a trusted counselor or other professional helpers to get the circular thought into horizontal position where it can be seen for what it really is. Self-knowledge can be constructively used to advantage if one knows where both the channels and the chasms are in his own existence. He becomes aware that others may have walked that way, too. The more one is aware and critical of self, the more he is willing to become aware of others and share their burdens. The more one is aware of self the less solidified the solutions.

This means, further, that the pastor can cultivate the capacity to be totally and brutally frank with himself. If he himself needs to talk about his deepest, inmost thoughts, the shared burden becomes more tolerable. He will recognize that this is the first principle in counseling—the sharing of burdens, beginning with one's own. This critical self-analysis is best gained through counseling or psychotherapy. Books are directional finders and can start the process. If he is to be of help, the pastor must have come to terms with his own existence, his past and his potential. He must have some kind of skills, which are being constantly sharpened at the wheel of experience. If his self-concept is sufficiently clear and his own thinking clarified as to his own identity, then he can proceed to be involved with others who are struggling with these life crises, including—and not exclusively—crises occasioned by grief.

How the pastor looks at death, as has been indicated, may also condition his response to calls for help in the grief process. How death appears to him, how he has dealt with death in his own immediate family may also tend to condition his attitudes. How he communicates the meaning of death in spoken or written word will also have its effect. If he minimizes its importance as a phase of existence, takes an unrealistic approach or tends to gloss over its impact, he may not only suppress the experience for another, but he may also suggest that he has not come to terms with his own potential terminal state. The tendency is not to look at it until it is upon one. Somehow the hope is cherished that maybe it is a long way off and "I'll not have to think about it until I have to."

"No man is an island," said John Donne, ". . . for every man's death diminishes me." This speaks to everyone, because death is a certain undeniable fact compelling choices of either hope or despair. The mystery, the burden of knowing one has to die, is a fact of existence. If what the modern existentialists tell us is true, the greatest threat experienced is the threat of *angst*—the threat of non-being, hence death.

Dr. Clemens Benda, Boston Psychiatrist, in his article "Bereavement and Grief Work,"[2] makes the same point: "The awareness of death in our own life—'being toward death!' as Martin Heidegger (German existential psychiatrist) says—gives life the consciousness of finity and poses the question of what to do with one's own life and what will happen afterward, into our own awareness."[3]

This wrestling with the problem of death in our own situation as well as that of another cannot be dismissed easily. We are confronted not only with our own feelings, but also with the feelings of others which need to be resolved before the pastor can be in a helping relationship. This is the role with which the pastor is charged.

---

[2] Paper given on October 18, 1961, at the University of Buffalo School of Medicine at a meeting sponsored by the Chaplains Department, Council of Churches of Buffalo and Erie County, and the Erie-Niagara Funeral Directors Association. Reprinted from *The Journal of Pastoral Care*, XVI, No. 1 (Spring 1962), 1–13.

[3] *Ibid.*, p. 9.

Occasionally it is discharged with some pious, impersonal, somewhat detached feeling: somehow this is all a bit unreal, impersonal, happening to the other fellow; let's get it over with and go on to some more agreeable tasks.

Many times the pastor's own view of death or his remembrance of poignant grief can become carried over into the relationship with the grief sufferer. This is the emotional freight he carries from the past that is never discharged and most likely will color his feeling and thinking and acting. This is most graphically illustrated by a pastor who grappled with the problem in terms of his own death. Though he was a very young person, relatively speaking, in the ministry, there was a morbid preoccupation with his own death. He had set up a neat defensive system and was not overly concerned. Nonetheless he had made out a last will and testament with elaborate details about his final disposition. It was to be shrouded in mystery, with no burial in the usual sense. After he had been spirited away from the deathbed there was to be a rough pine box, no ceremony, and everything over with quickly. No one was to mourn him. There was to be a simple memorial service afterward. All was to be light and hope and the Christian's promise of immortality. There was to be no mourning or tears because the Christian has been relieved of that necessity. This was an attempt on his part not to spend too much money on a funeral. It also stemmed from some erroneous impression concerning the greedy preoccupation of funeral directors to milk his parishioners. He was not going to let that happen; he was going to make it known that this was the way one arranged the funeral. This pastor had had a bad experience, a residual carry-over from the time when his mother died and he was unable to resolve the grief in his own situation. Anything associated with grief, death, or funerals, therefore, had a bad connotation. He was determined to push it back as far from his consciousness as he could. It is almost a foregone conclusion that until he faces and resolves the issue of grief for himself he will scarcely be in a position to minister effectively to others in the throes of grief. The necessity of coming to terms with the basic issues of one's own existence was never more demonstrably clear.

How then does a pastor go about relating to his parishioners who experience the profound phenomenon of death and grief? If his seminary training helped him to actualize the experience of death or to deal with the grief sufferer, he is most fortunate. It has been the experience of most pastors that this has been ignored or even glossed over in the courses in practical theology. Unless he had clinical training or has been exposed to the problem of suffering, death, and grief by taking an internship in a parish setting, he has gone to his task without much preparation for dealing with the grief syndrome. The seminary assumed that he was going to get this experience on the job, as with many of the other practical tasks of the ministry. Some can recall the utter aloneness they experienced when they made their first call upon the members of a family where death had just occurred. They will remember the awkwardness of their attempt to comfort the family suffering a profound sense of loss, and the hollowness of stumbling through some familiar words of Scripture and a prayer. In spite of this, the family was appreciative of the pastor's being there. That's all that really counted, that he was there for whatever support they derived from that moment.

To minister helpfully to the grief sufferer, the pastor needs to know his parishioner, as redundant as this may sound, as well as his personal history. If the relationship has been close, if he has stood by in the terminal illness, if he has visited regularly in the hospital or home, then there is more likelihood of trust and confidence. The family will more naturally lean upon him in the crisis situation because he has stood by during other trials and vicissitudes. He needs to be aware that they have been hurt and may be weeping, stunned, blocked, silent, withdrawing, agitated, or chattering incessantly. He enters into the relationship knowing that this family will have to be seen and treated as individuals, each with his own peculiar particular reaction to the grief situation. He goes knowing that he may receive some personal abuse, not really meant for him. It is possible that he may hear the seething denunciation of God for allowing this to happen, or some hostility directed either toward the doctor for failure to prevent the death or, in fact, toward anyone whom the family feels failed to function properly. There is anger at the fact that they are forced into a situation beyond restoration or restitution. The pastor goes knowing that he may be or become a crutch, someone to lean on, a guide, a companion. He goes knowing that the power to soothe and to relieve is required.

Some pastors come away from these encounters visibly moved and a bit shaken because so much is vested in them as a person. The pastor will know that they may expect him to be there, even to help with the arrangements, to take over because the family may not be able to function adequately. He enters the process of grief in these earliest moments. These moments can be best utilized not as the occasion for spouting pious phrases, but to prepare the bereaved for the grief work necessary before he can be free from the burden, which at this time seems to be almost insurmountable. The pastor may feel the necessity for spiritual-emotional undergirding himself in order to be equal to the meaningful experience of setting the tone and the atmosphere for the days, weeks, and months ahead.

Being knowledgeable about the family may be of primary importance, but in his attempt to be helpful the pastor may unwittingly or unknowingly prevent the person(s) from moving ahead toward acceptance of the fact of death. Supercilious reassurance such as, "John will be better off," "He's gone to his eternal rest," "God wanted him," "The baby is even now with God," or "You have sent an angel to heaven," are attempts to avoid coming to grips with the acceptance of the fact that John is dead! Pastors have even fallen into the practice of avoiding the use of the word *death* by saying, "He departed this life," "He's passed away," "He has entered into rest," or "He's gone to his eternal reward." (Maybe his widow thinks he went to hell and he deserved it!) The pastor may be using faulty reassurance, which is an attempt by the reassurer to reassure himself. This is the so-called *silver cloud approach*, which tends to cover up rather than to release feelings. If the pastor is uncomfortable—and no one is ever comfortable in the presence of death or loss—in the grief situation, this is communicated. He may need to keep talking in order not to be embarrassed by the awkward silences or the profusion of tears. He may say things like: "There, there now, things are not so bad; John wouldn't have wanted you to cry." The pastor needs to be able to say: "Would you like to talk about it?" or "Tell me how things are!" If this has not been his usual approach he may feel equally uncomfortable, but if he is to help his parishioner with grief work, he must enable the sufferer to tell of his loss—his story in his own way and in his own words. This generally provides the initial release of feelings. One does not have to pretend that it doesn't hurt or that the loss is not as great as it is. This is the only way one can begin to realize the loss and begin to take the road to acceptance of the pain of it.

The rehearsal of the events of the days preceding the death is usually a good place to begin the process of grief work. As the story is told over and over again it has a cathartic effect upon the teller. It becomes easier to tell and thus easier, eventually, to bear. The acceptance is also begun in this way. One has seen this many times in the funeral home, where the survivors hear condolences spoken and where they can speak to those who come to share these moments of sorrow. A professional man who lost his son in a tragic accident, while he stood beside the casket was gradually better able to actualize the loss as he was telling the events, the last conversation, the hopes he had cherished for the son's future. This was real tragedy with poignant memory of how things were and how they might have been. His talking about these things was a necessary step in readjustment. Fortunate is the person who has friends who offer more than the hand of sympathy.

The sufferer needs those who will listen with deep and abiding concern, who will empathize, which is more than to sympathize. To sympathize means to feel along with; to empathize (from the German *einfühling*) means to feel into the situation of someone else in such a positive way that the individual knows that there is someone who walks with him, who knows the hurt and the painful reminders of days that used to be, who is standing by. To empathize may be difficult. The pastor has been taught to be a dispenser of answers, mostly, as Reuel Howe affirmed, "to answer questions people aren't asking." When the pastor comes in face-to-face relationship he needs to be aware that words aren't important, but that being there, involved in his parishioner's situation, is more important; to stand where he stands. There is an old Indian expression which affirms that before you can know what another person experiences, you have to "walk in his moccasins."[4] To *be*, more than to do or

---

[4] Harper Lee makes the same point in the Pulitzer prize novel *To Kill A Mockingbird* (Philadelphia: J. B. Lippincott Co., 1960). It concerns the defense of a Negro unjustly accused. The central character, a lawyer, comes to this point in his own thinking and is then able to defend his client.

say, makes the pastor a symbol of Him who came to share the burdens of others.

Real empathy begins by entering into meaningful dialogue with another. It becomes the key to unlock doors closed to most outsiders. It is an active process of being there—to be able to go where the sufferer wants to go, to be able by standing there to communicate *I understand*, without saying so in so many words. It is like feeling the emotional pulse of a patient without touching him. Not too much attention has been given to the symbolic role of the pastor or to his empathetic role. Practicing the presence of quietness in bearing and attitude creates the atmosphere in which another can begin to unburden himself, as the ancient collect says, "unto whom all things are known and from whom no secrets are hid."

CHAPTER THREE

PASTORAL TECHNIQUES
For GRIEF MANAGEMENT

The pastor ministering to the grief sufferer needs not only to know himself and be knowledgeable about the grief process, but also to have some "know-how" and mastery of the techniques. Of necessity, he will need to equip himself with a consistent, well-defined, usable methodology of counseling. Though he has no implements or tools in the usual sense of the word, he will find it helpful to re-ëxamine his usual approaches to persons in grief crises. His principles and practices of pastoral care, however, cannot be separated from other forms of crisis ministry, where faithful disciplined practice is requisite.

If he has not already, the pastor may profitably begin to master a methodology which can be applied in the numerous crises he faces daily. He is obliged to master one methodology before he can advance beyond it. He may never have been forced to go beyond superficial *one-shot* relationships because he has almost traditionally been pegged, knowingly or unknowingly, as a *giver of advice*—equal to any and all situations! This role is assumed by those who find it easier to tell others what to do than to counsel with them. Pastoral counseling requires a larger investment of time than some ministers feel they have to devote to it. In the larger parishes with heavily programmed activities, the minister may be able to give only a fraction of his time to a single individual. As one pastor of a large metropolitan church remarked regretfully, "I can give her some time today, but I don't know when I'll be able to set another appointment in the next two weeks."

To counsel means to deliberate together, usually over an indeterminate period of time. To be able to take the time, to schedule the hours, is essential to any sustaining, supportive relationship. Permissive counseling has not been the pastor's stock in trade, because it requires him to follow where the counselee (parishioner) leads.

In modern pastoral care the directive nature of the ministry is fading in favor of a broader concept of meeting the needs of the individual. Exhortation and directive counseling approaches are outmoded even though they are the usual tactic of those who have never really made a conscientious effort to examine what kind of methodology they are using or could use for the greatest benefit of the counselee.

Pastoral counseling is a difficult and demanding discipline. It involves a one-to-one relationship in which the pastor and parishioner work toward the solution or resolution of a problem, thus enabling the counselee to function better as a person. This also demands responsibility on the part of the pastor to utilize himself as a person and his skills in such a way as to allow the individual to grow at his own rate of speed, at the level of his own need. The pastor must know the rigors of such discipline so that he can be alert and aware of the human situation, so that he can be steeped in the ways of men.

Pastoral counseling is to the pastor what psychotherapy is to the psychiatrist. Sometimes pastoral counseling is not very curative, but it does not hold that it cannot, therefore, ever be effective. No one would argue that there is anything approaching universal competence. The pastor, however, may be the only one able to reach the grief sufferer because he stands in that unique position of *pastor*, and all that this rich word conveys. The relationship preceding the crisis may likely continue during and after the crisis, provided the pastor always has shown an interest in and concern for the individual.

The approach needs to be individualized. The person suffering pain of loss needs individual attention in direct proportion to the situation. He needs the support of someone, outside the family circle, upon whom he can depend. It seems redundant to say: treat the individual as an individual; but there is no recourse without doing violence to the "wholeness" concept of man. The ability of the pastor to help the grief sufferer will depend largely upon his endowment,

skills, and training. The pastor needs the kind of competence in dealing with individuals that every art demands of its practitioners.

In theological education more and more seminaries are requiring
clinical pastoral training before graduation, so that a fledgling pastor
can learn a methodology of counseling. By subjecting one's work to
supervision, he learns what works and what does not. This kind of
learning takes place in the controlled setting of an institution under
trained supervisor-chaplains. Major training groups offering this type
of practicum[1] are tying the practical aspects of the parochial task with
theological education in very definitive ways.

The pastor cannot desert the area of pastoral counseling or deny
that grief sufferers are his legitimate domain whether or not he has
been trained or has temperament for the task. He cannot default in
this ministry. This is part of the uniqueness of his role in the crisis
ministry he is called upon to render.

If the pastor is to be *there,* to be of aid to the grief sufferer, he
needs to develop philosophical, psychological, and practical ways to
get at the heart of interpersonal relationships. This is applicable in
all crisis ministries. These are not always as tangible as the tools of
the garage mechanic, but they are tools nonetheless. Among the basic
considerations are:

(1) A need to have a genuine love of persons for themselves. This
    is, again, what is meant by empathy. They need to be treated
    as persons and not as personages.[2]
(2) A need for practice in demonstrated skills, to use himself in
    such a way that he bears the burden of another without being
    overburdened.
(3) Beyond the workable methodology, a sensitivity to others. If
    the grief sufferer expresses hostility, what does this mean? If he
    wants to be bawled out, if he seems to be saying one thing and
    meaning another, is there the sensitivity of a photographic plate
    to pick up the shades of meaning?
(4) An awareness, further, of limitations. If the problem, the grief
    reaction being manifest, is beyond the scope of the pastor's
    ability, he needs to be able to refer tactfully to more adequate

---

[1] See *The Journal of Pastoral Care,* XVI, No. 4, (Winter 1962) and
Pastoral Psychology Magazine, Vol. 13, (January, 1963), for description and
location of Centers offering training.

[2] See Paul Tournier, *The Meaning Of Persons* (New York: Harper & Row,
Publishers, 1957).

help. He may have a tendency to refer too quickly because his own feelings may get mixed up with those of his parishioner. This means there is recognition on the pastor's part that some people don't want help even though he may be wringing out his heart and all overtures are rebuffed.

(5) A need, above all, to be a good listener.

To listen responsively has not always been the pastor's forte, since his basic training has placed a major emphasis upon preaching and teaching. In a nationwide survey done in connection with the author's dissertation[3] and a more recent survey done among the Canadian Lutheran Synod in 1961, the greatest percentage of pastors felt that preaching was the most essential task of the ministry. When asked, "Where do you find most of your opportunities for pastoral care?" the overwhelming majority said they came about as a result of calling, not preaching.

Disciplined listening or "directive listening," to use one of Russell Dicks' terms, is listening to encourage others to talk. This is an essential concern of the pastor in his primary role of allowing the grief sufferer to express his hurt and loss. Responsive listening or "responsive counseling,"[4] first coined by Paul Johnson, means responding to what the person (grief sufferer) says, hearing the meaning behind the words, catching the nuances and overtones.[5] The pastor who listens allows a person to tell his own story in his own way and to be heard without being condemned or condoned. If he listens permissively, he opens the way for the grief sufferer to tell his story and develop his own insights as quickly as he is able. This requires an attentive ear to be able to differentiate the shades of meaning, the foreboding silences. The pastor will listen in silence. If he is not disturbed by silences, they can be used creatively. The person may be trying to think through what he has been saying or to be able to respond to what has just been said. Listening is a sharing of burdens. A load is better carried by two. Confession, then, becomes the heart of good counseling.

Permissive counseling enables the counselee to release feelings, de-

---

[3] See *The Development of Lutheran Pastoral Care in America*, unpublished Doctoral dissertation, Boston University, 1949.

[4] Paul E. Johnson, *Psychology of Pastoral Care* (Nashville: Abingdon Press, 1953).

[5] *Ibid.*, p. 100.

velop new insights, and take on more responsibility for self-direction. He is allowed to say what he wants, knowing that he will be accepted without being forced to accept goals prescribed by the pastor. The development of one's insight is closely related to self-discovery. Insights cannot be transfused. They are an achievement from within, as the word implies. Responsibility for self-direction rests with the counselee. The pastor cannot take responsibility without sharing some of the blame. The person must grow at his own rate of speed, or he will become extremely dependent. The pastor needs to exercise disciplined self-control lest he talk too much or ask too many questions. He will be led to the most significant areas primarily when he is patient, concerned, and then able meaningfully to rephrase the essence of the grief sufferer's remarks. Rapport is not gained by recital of similar experiences. The pastor who talks about himself is digressing and diverts the emphasis toward himself. Pastoral counseling, like good conversation, is communication. The pastor does not steal the ball of conversation but tosses it back and forth in interchange that meaningfully captures what has been said and is being said.

To minister effectively to the grief sufferer or persons in any crisis, the pastor ought to be aware of the following techniques for grief management:

(1) Start with the person where he actually is, not where the pastor thinks he is or should be.
(2) Accept the person where he is, no matter whether the pastor agrees with the counselee's basic premises or not.
(3) Clarify feelings expressed to be better able to understand the feeling produced.
(4) Restate the sentence in part, or its essence. It is not so much a matter of repeating the previous sentence, rather something like: "If I get what you are saying . . . ," "You seem to be saying . . . ," or "From what I hear you say, you are telling me. . . ."
(5) Focus on choices; hold up alternative courses of action, if action is demanded. Let the counselee see for himself where each of the choices will lead.
(6) Interpret cautiously.
This is generally a concluding function although it can be utilized in the course of counseling when it seems to be appropriate, but rarely in a first counseling session.

The pastor must avoid certain pitfalls, if he is to be effective in the helping relationship:

(1) Avoid being a moral policeman. Judgmental attitudes tend to make the person run for cover.

(2) Respect the private world of the counselee. Each person has a right to be himself and show only that part of his inner self which he wants anyone else to see or to know about.

(3) Do not put your parishioner (counselee) on the defensive. If he has to put up neat defenses, he will avoid coming to grips with the basic issues of his existence.

(4) Do not preach to him.
All the facts need to be in before value judgments can be made. Allow the person to say: "I hated him for the way he treated me," or "I guess I was as much at fault as he was."

(5) Do not take sides.
Once the pastor takes sides he cannot retain objectivity; his prejudices will show.

(6) Do not assume the role of the questioner.
You may get the answer to the questions but nothing more.

(7) Do not rush things; there is no such thing as *quickie counseling*.

(8) Do not make rash statements or promises you can't keep.

(9) Keep confidences confidential.
There is nothing more devastating to an individual than to have his private conversation to the pastor repeated by someone else who could not possibly have known had the pastor kept quiet.

(10) Keep family and personal matters from infiltrating into the helping relationship and influencing courses of action. This takes the focus away from the person and fixes it on the pastor.

(11) Keep the language simple.
Avoid talking over the head of the person or using terms unfamiliar to him.

(12) Learn how to terminate a session.
This can be done by *structuring* in the beginning by saying such things as: "I have one hour to spend with you . . ." or "I can see you now, but my next appointment is at 2:00 P.M."

The primary aim in all pastoral counseling is to determine certain factors about the counselee. Is the individual able to go on from here with minimal help or with no further help required at this time? Is he a self-sustaining being? (This is not to be confused with the fact of our entire dependence on God.) Is he a self-activating being not needing to be pushed or shoved from outside or inside? Is he a free interacting being, capable of making choices by which he assumes responsibility for the way he is and the course of action decided upon?

Every pastor has his own unique way of approaching individuals. He may never have formulated his own working philosophy. If he had, he could put into words an operational way of handling his crisis ministries. A self-help check list for the pastor might include such questions as the following:

1. What am I trying to do in helping people?
2. What do my counselees expect from me?
3. Why do my counselees come to me?
4. How can I be of most help to the person?
5. How much time do I have to give to this individual?
6. How do I conceive my role?
7. What are my limitations?
8. Do I know the sources of referral in my community?
9. Can I make a diagnosis?
10. Do I need to succeed?

Such questions point up the necessity of having a usable, consistent methodology and approach to people. While it will be individualized, it can be used once it has become a part of the very being and life of the pastor.

Not every pastor will be able to take sufficient time away from his parish to take advanced clinical pastoral training. Few parishioners understand the necessity for further education and sharpening of the pastor's skills. Hopefully, after a period of training he will be better able to cope with the problems on a more adequate basis. Because one takes further training, however, does not offer any gilt-edged guarantee that the pastor will be any different if he does not have the capacity to assimilate and use the experience gained.

Permissive counseling allows the grief sufferer wide latitude in pursuing any avenue or area of his problem without being prodded or pushed in any direction. The pastoral counselor has to be secure enough in himself to allow individuals to choose their own course of action. He holds up his end of the problem while the individual is there. The counseling time is for the counselee to use as he chooses. No value judgments are made because the individual will, in the last analysis, remain dependent or move ahead as a result of his own choosing. The pastoral counselor *stands by* while the person doing the struggling leans on him for support. When he no longer needs the counselor, the counselor can walk away. Eventually, hopefully, the individual will be able to move freely on his own.

This methodology lends itself to *learning by doing, while doing.*[6] The outline for note writing, in the appendix, although used for hospital visitations, can be utilized for practice in writing up verbatim notes on selected patients or parishioners (grief sufferers). It would be ideal if the pastor could have someone who has had training, or if he were close enough to a Center where there is a trained chaplain-supervisor, who would be able to review and evaluate his work so that helpful direction might be given for future growth.

It will be acknowledged that the parish pastor has not been accustomed to writing notes, let alone writing down conversations in verbatim fashion, thereby subjecting his work to such scrutiny. If he can overcome the timidity he may have about committing to paper these personal conversations and practice this methodology faithfully for a specific period of time, he will be surprised at the difference it will make in his ability to help people struggling in grief crises situations that he encounters in his work-a-day world. He will find himself reaching a much deeper, more meaningful level.

The suggestion made here is that he try writing down, according to the formula, ten interviews with grief sufferers. The prediction is that, having worked faithfully with this method, he will render a more effective pastoral ministry.

After the pastor gets beyond this initial stage of verbatim writing he could then keep summary notes on subsequent visits. These notes would serve as a review and reminder of what transpired in the previous interviews. Gradually he would build up a sizable laboratory of experience for future reference and study.

If he is willing to practice this kind of discipline, it will redound to the benefit of his parish and the community in which he lives. Others may call upon him for help. He will feel more confident and competent in dealing with crises situations. A physician once said

---

[6] The author adapted these procedural steps from a seminar session with James Burns at Massachusetts General Hospital.

that if a pastor can work effectively with those in mourning he will have *earned his salt*.

We conclude with a recorded verbatim interview with a woman whose husband died rather suddenly. It can be only a partial example, to give some idea of how to get started.

INDENTIFYING INFORMATION: Mrs. Orr is a 48-year-old, white female, who was referred for consultation by her own pastor. She has two children, a girl 16 and a boy 13, who were adopted as infants. Her husband had died of a heart attack one year previous to her initial interview. The pastor had the funeral, and had followed the family for several months after the death of the husband. When she was referred, the oldest of the two siblings was having school problems. (This information was related by the pastor in a telephone conversation.)

When Mrs. Orr appeared at the chaplain's study, she was greeted by the chaplain-pastor and made to feel comfortable as each sized up the other.

P. Good morning Mrs. Orr. Your pastor said you would be here. Please come in. You take this chair and I'll sit here. (Offers chair seated opposite. He begins the conversation.) Now tell me what brought you to the Center.

Mrs. O. I guess Pastor Able told you about my husband's death.

P. Yes, he gave some of the information over the phone. Suppose you tell me how things are going now.

Mrs. O. I have had this awful feeling ever since Fred died a year ago of a heart attack. I feel I am here, yet detached. I get upset very easily and I am having difficulty sleeping at night. . . .

P. You are not able to function as you'd like to function, is that it?

Mrs. O. Yes, that's about it, I can't get to myself. I can't break out of it. I can't get released from me. (pause) I've been on some medication ever since the funeral.

P. You want to break out, but something keeps you from feeling free.

Mrs. O. It's like feeling trapped, like being in a cage. I tried to go to the camp that the Church runs, but that didn't help. I took a job, but I guess it was too soon. I sort of had this ringing in my head as if it were going click, click . . . I just can't seem to get going or get interested in anything.

P. You've tried, but you just don't get anywhere.

Mrs. O. Pastor Able tried to help. I originally went to see him about my daughter. She took it pretty hard when my husband died. I went to see him about myself, too. I knew I should be doing better. It is a strange feeling to realize he wasn't there. I was scared to live, afraid to die. It was a frightening ordeal. It can't be so . . . but he's gone. . . .

(She went on to talk about her difficulties with daughter in the school situation in a sort of rambling fashion as she recalled the days before and after her husband's death. She then talked about her own background, filling in some of the details of her own teen-age development and a significant event that occurred when she was age 15. Her younger brother had died and she described it as "just like losing a part of me." The thread is picked up here, again, by the pastor-counselor.)

P. Your husband's death reminded you of this previous loss.

Mrs. O. The bottom just dropped out. My husband had been ill most of our married life. I anticipated that this could happen for such a long time that I was in a kind of stupor. The nurse gave me something to take. I went through the funeral real well. I steeled myself; I didn't let myself go. I didn't cry at the funeral. My back felt like it was going to crush from holding it up.

P. You weren't able to express what you were feeling.

Mrs. O. It was his funeral. It wasn't any place for me to let go or to break down.

(Mrs. O. went on to say that her husband was a good churchman. It was a good time for him to die, but it was a sad time for her, she said.)

She always gets this way around the Christmas season because her husband died the day after Christmas and her brother and her mother-in-law also died close to the end of the year. She always anticipated something happening at this time of year. We talked near the end about what she wanted to do about facing up to this grief situation and she said she wanted to face it and to go on living and to make the best home for her teen-agers. She recognized it was going to be a struggle and she was going to need help.

It was our feeling after seeing her that her own pastor could deal with her in a supportive way, offering her weekly interviews to come in and talk about this. This was done. She had begun to assimilate and accept the loss. At one period in the readjustment she voluntarily admitted herself to the State Hospital, but is now back in the community. As far as the pastor is concerned she is making satisfactory progress.

This is a brief example of verbatim interview with a grief sufferer, chosen mostly to illustrate how one utilized permissive counseling in getting at the real feelings of the sufferer, and recording it in verbatim fashion to take a look at technique.

This interview took place one year after the death of husband. She was still not able to accept the loss or move far from the center of her depressive mood. The physician who had been treating her husband was also feeding her tranquilizers. She was still on them at the time of the interview. It was our conclusion that she had not faced the full impact of her husband's death and had yet to assimilate the loss.

CHAPTER FOUR

CONSTRUCTIVE And DESTRUCTIVE WAYS
Of HANDLING GRIEF

"Pastor, it hurts!" The tears streaming down her cheeks gave every indication that she was in extreme discomfort, as if someone had dealt a sharp blow to the midriff. The loss of her husband was being transmitted into physical, experiential pain. If you had asked her where it hurt, she would have told you, "Inside." The only outward manifestation of the hurt, the sorrow in this case, was the tears. This was pain of loss being demonstrated externally. Pain infiltrates the tissues because the psychomotor parts of the brain are reacting to the stimulus of loss, irrefutable loss. There is discomfiture in pain. It isolates the sufferer from all others. The sufferer concludes that no one can really experience the pain as he does. Pain has a hypnotic effect on the sufferer, much like a moving pendulum with its rhythmic monotonous movements, when it seems like it will never end. It has been described as having a numbing effect. It is unbearable, unendurable, and at times interminable.

The writer called upon a woman in the hospital who had been badly burned. She had lost three children in a flash fire in her home. After rescuing one infant, she was driven back in an attempt to save the three helpless children trapped in the upper bedroom. She sustained burns over 90 percent of her back and described her pain as unyielding except for the injections of morphine which brought temporary relief. At other times the pain was overwhelming—taking over until she hardly knew if the power within would sustain her. She was drawn into the "hypnotic orbit of possessive pain" with the burden of both physical and psychic pain which could not be erased in the battle she waged for life. She cried out in endless nights of agony like Rachel of old who wept because her children were no more.

1. *Feelings Need To Be Expressed.* One prerequisite in handling grief is the expression of feeling. It is of paramount importance to be able to say it hurts, to feel the hurt keenly to the very depth of one's being, and to be able to express this openly and unashamedly before someone who understands. Where this open expression is not allowed and the hurt is glossed over, the person is heading for trouble. We speak of ventilation of feelings as having a cathartic effect. To be able to get it up and get it out or to be able to discharge the feeling before it has assumed an engulfing character releases pent-up feeling. Confession produces the same effect. To be able to get the bottled-up emotion out into the open, to unburden oneself, is to feel relieved. It may not make the burden any lighter; it will still have to be borne. The pain of loss will still have to be faced, but some of the sting will be removed as the grief sufferer is allowed this kind of expression.

2. *Facts Need To Be Faced.* The fact of one's existence must be faced squarely, without flinching. There is no dodging the issues of life and death, not only the fact of another's death but also the fact of one's own death. These realities are faced each time someone closely related dies. It is the stiff, unbending truth of the matter that is hard to accept. The mother, father, sisters, and brothers of a twin son and brother who was struck and killed by a hit-and-run driver must face the fact that Mark will no longer occupy the familiar chair—his usual place in the family circle. This has to be accommodated eventually in the daily existence of the family, minus one.

3. *Pain And Loss Need To Be Accepted.* One does not have to do the accepting immediately. Grief work—that is, working through the death or loss—may not necessarily have a time limit set upon it. Observers have maintained that from three to six months is a normal period for acceptance of the idea of the loss. The time when it begins to be accepted into the pattern of daily routine may be the initial period, but this does not mean necessarily that the individual sufferer will not have moments of pain. The actualizing of the loss, through death or separation, impinges upon him. The moment he hears of the death of someone else, reads about a divorce, hears about a plane crash in a distant city, comes upon a faded love letter, fingers the pages of an old picture album, or observes a mother kissing a child

good-by he may be poignantly reminded of the way things were. He still must come to terms with his grief by accepting things as they are now, or never fully and finally resolve for himself the loss.

4. *The Need For Assimilation Of The Fact Of Loss In Daily Living.* Having accepted loss through death or other sustained kinds of loss, there is the need to assimilate the fact into one's existence, to begin to be able to act appropriately, to be oneself again, to regain equilibrium as quickly as time permits, to rejoin groups and join in with other persons again in the constant interaction of life with all of its interpersonal encounter. It is essential to resume quickly old duties, or to assume new ones—but not too quickly. Sometimes a person will take a flight into health, throw himself into activity just for the sake of activity. He will attempt to blunt the pain of the loss by endless and repetitious being on the go, fearing if he were to stop and catch his breath he would fold up. Some have the feeling that they must become the ambassadors of the deceased to carry out death-bed requests. In the more morbid reactions, carrying out such wishes can have bizarre consequences, as in the case of the woman in Chapter One who would not bury her mother because she had expressed a senile death wish never to be buried.

5. *Need For Protective Layers.* No one can predict in advance how long the process of the assimilation of loss will take. This is an individual matter. Some people, especially those from closely knit families, are able to make a more rapid recovery. If there is a strong solidarity within the ethnic, social, or cultural group, it provides the necessary insulation and support for lessening the blow while not making light of it. Similarly, in any break in an important relationship (separation, divorce, reactive depression, crises of any sort), the protective layer surrounding the individual helps with the process of assimilation. It can be thought of in terms of a circle with a central core, the individual cell of civilization being in the center and additional bands such as immediate family, relatives and friends, helping specialists, and the community at large surrounding the nucleus. As long as there are adequate substitutes, the break—the loss—is more manageable.

As in any suffering, one can accommodate the loss when others are standing by to help. While the immediate family may be supportive, they may be wrestling with their own reactions. Often it is

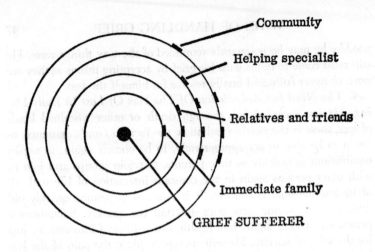

- Community
- Helping specialist
- Relatives and friends
- Immediate family
- GRIEF SUFFERER

the helping specialists who are called upon to fill the gap, to apply the *emotional tourniquet*. Here is where the pastor can begin to fill the role of therapist, not in the medical, technical sense, but as his title implies, as a healer. The pastor needs to follow through, making periodic visits in order to be of maximal help. He fulfills his role by being at the first aid stations in life. He is available when all the dust has dissipated after the funeral, after the loss has occurred.

6. *The Need To Verbalize Feelings.* If the pastor is willing to allow the person to verbalize his feelings, the bitter gall may be drained off and healing balm may be poured into the wounds. Pastoral listening becomes important: (1) to hear the recital of events; (2) to rehearse the last moments; (3) to review the past accomplishments; (4) to discover those facts that have meaning for the person; and (5) to provide the atmosphere for this release. All of these are necessary steps in the process of verbalization by the grief sufferer. This is his grief work!

7. *The Need To Explore Alternative Courses Of Action.* The pastor may be able to assist with the successful management of grief if he is able to help the individual grief sufferer explore alternative courses of action so that a workable plan may be formulated for his future. The pastor is in the best position to follow each course of action to a possible logical outcome, still allowing the grief sufferer to choose—not pushing for one course as opposed to another. The grief sufferer may be stalled on the track, unable to move in any di-

rection. He should not be pushed too strongly. The pressure of the pastor's presence may be enough to move the person off dead center. The interest and concern manifested will be appreciated because the pastor merely stood by. Ultimately there is realization of need for readjustment of one's mode of living, of the necessity to find avenues for expression of one's own creativity.

A pastor, knowing his community (parish), may also know of others who have successfully worked through these crises experiences and may do no more than put them in touch with each other.

8. *Need For Community: Grief Anonymous.* If the pastor has in his congregation a group of people, a core group, who have worked through their own grief, he might, with a little coaching, provide people who would act as buffers—creating the kind of buffer relationship that would help fellow grief sufferers build bridges of new relationship. The pastor could, if he were willing, form a group of people who have worked through the experience of grief and who would contact the family or individual within a week after the loss has occurred. He will encourage them to keep in touch with the grief sufferer, especially if there are those who do not seem to be responding well. The person who has actually managed his own grief situation may act as a cushion to help the grief sufferer by providing someone to whom he can relate.

One aspect of this type of buffer relationship is being successfully carried out in some places by a newly formed national organization called Parents Without Partners.[1] The groups were formed for the purpose of providing a common meeting ground for those who have suffered loss of a partner through death, separation, or divorce. Its primary purpose is not to find partners, though this often happens, but to provide a group experience in which problems related to the grief experience can be aired and feelings clarified in an atmosphere in which everyone has similar experiences to bring to the collective gathering. When the writer addressed a local chapter, the group had not considered their experience as being synonymous with the grief syndrome. They were more concerned with preventative measures. They expressed such concerns as: How does one raise children, be-

---

[1] Parents Without Partners, Inc., 80 Fifth Avenue, New York, New York.

ing mother and father? and What could they do to avoid the recurrence of their predicament? They had not begun to face up to their losses, but seemed to be searching for answers to questions in their individual existences. This kind of group could be utilized, under proper leadership, to explore avenues of readjustment to meaningful existence. They will have to get beyond the group to come to grips, individually, with their own unique situations. Pastors could become involved with these groups in helpful ways by providing meeting space, acting as individual counselors to these persons, and involving other helping specialists. In this way they would assist the grief sufferers in finding direction for their lives.

9. *Need For Relatedness.* Grief sufferers are in need of relatedness not only to fellow grief sufferers but also to the community at large. To state it another way, there is the need for finding creative fulfillment. Death or other significant losses mean the eventual need for finding one's own niche. There is need to live out life's role with some degree of satisfaction. For example, after one is free from the image of the deceased and the business affairs are in some semblance of order, the need is to find some useful purpose, cause, or relationship to which one can give oneself. This involves an act of will and commitment. Human beings do have a large degree of resilience, or bounce-back power. One never really knows how much reserve potential he has until he is called upon to use it. Few really tap the depth of the wellsprings or power sources that they have within themselves.

Finding new meaning in one's existence begins with the recognition that there are tasks to be done, new goals to reach, new patterns to be established, new roles to be played. One cannot run away from life forever. One can be on a vacation for only a limited period. He comes to the point at which he must take individual responsibility for self-direction. Potential reservoirs are untapped. Everyone is important to at least one other person. The want ads in every newspaper are signposts for finding new outlets. Friends, relatives, the pastor may be among those knowing of some employer who is looking for the kind of talent or skill possessed by the grief sufferer that can be utilized. A new goal may be the taking up of an old job, following one's profession again, finding a new occupation, or going back to school in order to increase earning power.

10. *A Need To Be Needed.* The nurse whose husband died found

her old supervisor needed someone to work the "graveyard shift." She saw the need for her to be needed. All it took was a slight push in the direction of the hospital. While breaking into the new routines, learning new medicines, and having a regular schedule were taxing at first, she found fulfillment because not only did someone find her, but she found herself. She became important in the scheme of things in hospital care and assumed the role of a respected and responsible nurse. She found in doing something for others that she was doing more for herself. She broke out of the shell she had thrown around herself and began to find new enthusiasm for life, a role to perform, a calling to fulfill, something to which she could give herself. This is what our Lord was saying about finding one's life by losing oneself. To strike out in a new venture may produce anxiety, but not to make the attempt is to lose one's purpose for living.

In time the greater majority of people usually make these adjustments. It does, however, take time and effort. There are really no short cuts to satisfying goals. No one is really ever spared going through the process of grief work. This is what Mrs. Dale was saying one day when we had our usual corridor conversation.

A Case In Point

Mrs. Dale is a hospital employee whose husband died suddenly of a *cerebral vascular accident* while they were on a vacation trip. When we first learned about his death we offered the usual condolences after her return to work. Not much more was said during the ensuing months, but each day one observed her manifesting signs of healthy readjustment—at least outwardly. Since she knew this book was in preparation she agreed to talk about her own grief reaction. She came to my office not long afterward and we had a lengthy discussion of her husband's death.

His death had occurred about ten months previous. She was far enough away from it to be in reasonable control of her emotions and seemed quite willing to tell how she felt about her grief reaction, as she said, "if it will help someone else." When I asked her to tell me about the way she was able to work through her grief, she said it wasn't easy at the beginning. They had only been married about a year and a half. This was a second marriage for both. "I had a feel-

ing of being numb for three or four days." Because of the sudden-
ness she was in a state of shock. Her reality testing was quite blunted.
The secondary reactions came also like shock waves. "I wanted to
rebel. It was like a sharp pain . . . The sharp part is gone now, but
I don't think I'll ever get over it entirely, because we were just beginning to enjoy life. . . ."

Review of past events. She then began to review the events
leading up to his death—what they had done together. The sudden
demise made the memory that much more poignant. Seven years had
elapsed between her first and second marriages. Her first husband
had been twenty years older than she and had been in ill health the
last few years of their life together. His death came as release. "I
realized part of my life was over . . . I had to start again, I had lost
a part of me . . ." This was true in the present circumstance. She
went on to say: "I had to take the risk of a second marriage . . .
there was such a short time, I really wasn't prepared for his
death. . . ."

Acceptance. "It's hard to point to a time when I really accepted
it. I'm not so sure I have made that stick . . . You say: 'Thy will be
done,' and then things begin to happen; you have to be careful what
you ask the Lord for . . . Death is not the worst thing; there are
things that are worse . . . But life goes on, nobody can really reassure you, you have to believe there is more to life than existence
here . . . Nothing I read helped very much, you just have to accept
it . . . At first I asked why? why? and no answers came . . . The
Twenty-third Psalm was so calming. It was used in the funeral service. It was the only thing I remember about the funeral service . . .
I kept using it over and over again . . . I don't mean it was the only
thing. The friends who came to call at the funeral home—this was
good and important, just the fact that they were there. They took the
time; they made an appearance and I was able to tell them what had
happened. The sudden shock of things coming to a halt." These days
were spent in receiving community support from those who had an
empathetic concern. She regretted that she hadn't taken enough time
off after the funeral before she went back to the routine of work, but
she affirmed that people should keep busy. Without something to

which to give herself she said she would have felt lost. There are times in an empty house, mostly on weekends and nights, that are hard to take. "I have never cried easily. I didn't very often in front of people, but when I was alone the tears came. . . . I felt like a stone . . . I do have the faith to carry me through these days . . . I like to talk about him; it doesn't disturb me now. I remember the good relationship we had. . . ."

Not all persons can work through the loss of loved ones as did Mrs. Dale; not all persons will. While percentages are not always statistically provable there are always a certain number in any group who have difficulty adjusting to life's crises. In all likelihood, in almost any congregation, about one of four persons will have more pronounced reactions, often in a distorted form. This is seen in the more morbid reactions. The defenses raised to protect the self from the threat to existence sometimes take on bizarre and undifferentiated patterns.

Destructive Ways Of Handling Grief

A common phenomenon is the delaying of taking any action—not to show any outward manifestation until a later date when the behavior seems inappropriate to outside observers. The grief sufferer may go through the whole experience without too much concern about what is going on around him, seemingly facing up to the situation, having all the religious resources available, and then suddenly at the death of another person he may have a grief reaction disproportionate to his involvement or relationship with the deceased. Even the death of an animal may cause such a person to weep copious tears, obviously meant for the former situation.

1. *Overactivity.* Sometimes, the reaction will be one of overactivity, throwing oneself into the stream of things with utter abandonment. This is a form of denial of grief. Busyness is an attempt to be evasive about the loss. It is sometimes a senseless, aimless wandering about, in dread of having to face the grim reality. There are attempts to blot out the image of the deceased. Often all pictures will be discarded or burned or hidden from sight—to destroy the evidence so to speak. Some will get rid of anything that is a reminder of the former relationship, sometimes to such an extent as to completely

obliterate any trace. The dramatic gesture seems only to accentuate the loss more keenly.

2. *Taking On Physical Symptoms.* Another kind of reaction is seen where the grief sufferer will take on the physical problem or last illness of the deceased. The person may develop heart trouble, or run from doctor to doctor suspecting a specific disease and never quite be reassured. The common symptoms are in the category known as psychosomatic disorders, and they may be markedly similar to the symptoms of such diseases as arthritis, rheumatism, colitis, and especially ulcerative colitis. These may be introjected, that is, taken over by the survivors, because this is their attempt at identification. They may take the same medicine, or individual characteristics may be incorporated by the grief sufferer such as adapting the same mannerisms or way of speaking.

3. *Withdrawal From Social Relationships.* A manifestation of distorted grief reaction may also be seen in the avoidance of social contact, especially any activity in which the deceased had participated or which the deceased and survivor shared together. It may also be related to occupation, where the survivor may attempt to take up the occupation of the deceased and fail miserably. The survivor may also enter into activities that may prove economically and socially disastrous. The person may give money away, not spoken of before in wills, or may enter into business ventures that are not financially sound. The grief sufferer may also be drawn into the hands of entrepreneurs who may rob him/her of both fortune and future.

Situations Demanding Psychological Or Psychiatric Help

There are some grief situations that may be beyond the ability and knowledge of the pastor to deal with effectively. Though he will not withdraw his supportive role, the pastor will refer the grief sufferer to a competent psychiatrist or member of the mental health team in the community, when and if they are available. The pastor will still stand by the grief sufferer in the relationship so that he will realize he is not alone. Some of these situations are: (1) the extreme depressive reaction or melancholia; (2) psychotic breaks with reality; and (3) suicidal tendencies. The latter is not always easy to spot or ferret out because the individual may not telegraph the danger signals in ordinary conversation. If the grief sufferer does not seem to be responding to ordinary measures involved in supportive relationship or structured counseling (where both pastor and counselee recognize the need), referral should be made, if available.

In considering suicidal tendencies it is significant to note that this problem is becoming one of national proportions when annually more than 25,000 persons in the United States die as a result of death by their own hands. As Farberow and Shneidman declare in their book by the same name, attempted suicide is *The Cry For Help*.[2] The pastor often feels powerless in dealing with the suicide, even though he may have a strong relationship with the person. The grief situation is sometimes so overwhelming that suicide offers the only alternative solution.

In the press, recently, a small clipping gave a trenchant reminder of this event which occurs over and over again. It told the story of a father whose eight-year-old daughter had been killed in an accident. He grieved inconsolably, deeded over an apartment building and house to the Church in her memory, and then finally shot himself. The untold agony, the mental anguish he suffered, pushed him to the breaking point. Even when the pastor is trying to help he may not be able to get close to the grief sufferer because the person makes himself inaccessible and rebuffs all efforts. The clergyman who accepts responsibility for potential suicides may have some of his own feelings involved if this person commits the fatal act. There are ultimate risks that have to be taken when one is involved with people in crises situations.

Potential Danger Signals In Grief Reactions

The following are some of the potential danger signals: (1) when someone feels he is no longer of value as a person; (2) when he acts in a manner inconsistent with his usual behavior; (3) when he makes veiled threats at self-destruction; (4) when he makes dramatic gestures through superficial attempts; (5) when he exhibits anti-social behavior; (6) when excessive hostility is demonstrated; (7) when he engages in excessive drinking; (8) when he is extremely

[2] Norman L. Farberow and Edwin S. Shneidman, *The Cry For Help* (New York: McGraw-Hill, Inc., 1961).

moody; (9) when he withdraws completely and no longer interacts with others; (10) when he is fleeing reality by sudden decisions to fly to remote places.

All these danger signals are indications that all is not working out well, that the grief sufferer is acting in such a way as not to be in control of his faculties or self. Then the pastor may be the only person who can reach into the situation and either help the family to take responsibility or, in consultation with members of the family, persuade the person to accept other professional help voluntarily. The family physician is in a position not only for consultation but also, by his authority and position in the community, for directing the plans that may have to be made.

Unrealistic Behavior

Unrealistic behavior may be masked because the person's defenses are intact. This became apparent in a counseling relationship with a woman who consulted our Counseling Center for help. What was a marital difficulty on presentation erupted dramatically from beneath the surface into a clear-cut case of unresolved grief. Mrs. Harris, a 33-year-old mother of two children, married for 12 years, found herself in love with another man and could not find her way out of the situation. Even though she had every material comfort, she lacked fulfillment. She stated that her husband failed to understand her and was of no help in her attempt to find herself and at the present moment she sees no future with her husband. Material poured forth rather spontaneously regarding the accidental death of a brother some twenty years previously, when she was 13 years old. She shut that door in her life and hasn't been able to open it since. She could not grieve at his funeral, nor was she able to express her grief outwardly with tears appropriate to the loss. She threw a shell around herself in such a way that, as she said, "Nobody reached me and I didn't reach anyone else." It was a year later, just before she entered high school, that she withdrew completely and was out of school for a year. Though she was never hospitalized and was cared for at home she only went through the motions of living. "My friends and teachers would come . . . they stood more like shadows than people." No one knows exactly what brought her out of her despondency. She said she wasn't sure she had ever really gotten all the way out. She did not come to marriage "as a well person." "When he [her brother] died I knew I would never love again because I didn't want to be hurt." She depended strictly on herself. She said she couldn't depend on her parents—they might be taken—and from that moment on felt that she had to stand on her own two feet.

Because her brother died suddenly in a car accident she couldn't tell him she did love him and felt guilty about this. "All I know is, after he died I didn't want to love anyone, perhaps I never loved anyone. I kept closing doors. . . ." These doors, she maintained, were kept closed until a certain man in town where she lived walked into her life and "I loved for the first time, but I really haven't found myself and I'm terribly insecure. . . ." As she recalled the daily memories associated with her brother in the counseling relationship over a period of several weeks, she stopped mourning her brother and crying when she picked up a newspaper and read about another accident. "My brother came back in this man, I had my brother back . . . My mother and sister said Brother came back to them in a dream . . . but my brother is real in this man, I knew why I loved this man so much even though he wasn't like my brother . . ."

This is a long and complicated case. One has no trouble seeing that the unrealistic behavior, the infidelity is related to brother's death. She began rationalizing her desire to leave husband in favor of a man who reminded her of the love of brother whom she lost. She could not get the insight that this was what was happening. She still wants to dissolve her relationship with her present husband. The only thing that keeps this from happening is that the wife of the man whom she somehow thinks is her brother reincarnated will not give her husband up to this irrational impulse resulting from someone's unresolved grief.

Unresolved grief, like unconfessed sin, has a way of complicating life. It may be insidious in its dimensions and produce untold heartache and anxiety. In this case, it affects two families and five children who are likely to be in need of help, themselves, unless the situation can be satisfactorily resolved. It is taxing to the ingenuity and skill of any pastoral counselor to continue working with this woman and her husband. Countless hours and much effort will have to be spent. It is the only way, in the long run, that a pastor can justify his existence as helper. If he can help only one such person to find integration and insight and health again he may become a workman who need not be ashamed.

The pastor must be aware: (1) that grief has a constructive function to perform, but it can be destructive in devastating dimensions; (2) that there is a process called grief work, which no one is spared; (3) that the part the pastor plays has a great deal to do with how soon and how well the grief sufferer faces the reality of death and other significant losses.

CHAPTER FIVE

WHEN GRIEF IS DENIED

Or DELAYED

Grief is like a time bomb; it is set to go off when detonated. It sometimes goes off unexpectedly and in most unusual ways, particulary when the timing device has been tampered with. It can explode with as much fury as any stored-up energy. Grief, like other emotions denied outlet, can go off in the most devastating fashion. When denied or delayed the effect is disturbing. The grief sufferer who denies grief may *never* come to grips with the reality of critical loss; whereas the grief sufferer who delays coming to grips is merely postponing the inevitable. It also has to be said that a denied emotion is also a delayed emotion; it will take its toll in other ways. The grief sufferer may feel that he can put off his grief if he doesn't acknowledge that the event happened or that the loved one really died. Such statements as: "I do not feel that he is gone" and "He is right here with me, by my side," are denials of reality. "He is not really dead; he has just gone to sleep" and "I keep setting his place as if he were just coming home from work" are denials of the fact of death, and reflect one's desire to hold on to the image. The following cases illustrate the powerful pull of both denial and delay. The first is that of a parish pastor. The facts of both denial and delay were clearly manifest, as he tried valiantly to struggle with the distinct losses of two persons close to him, a small infant and subsequently his first wife. The losses appeared as isolated incidents until he began to talk about them. Then the evidence pointed in the direction of a somewhat closer parallel than appeared on the surface. The *fuse* was lit rather accidentally.

59

The Case of Mr. Clarke—*Identifying data*:

Mr. Clarke is a young pastor in his early forties, married for the second time. There were three children by his first wife and one by his second. He has been married seven years; his previous marriage was of five years' duration. He is a well-trained, capable pastor of a fairly substantial congregation, in a large metropolitan area. Energetic and able, he drives himself with a passion that leaves little time for recreation. Though he seems always to be in a hurry, it is a cover up, apparently for an aggressive drive which he has. Long, arduous tasks and challenges are his special forte. If you want to get something accomplished, he's the type of person you would call on. Looking at him objectively, from all outward appearances he is a man in a hurry, a man with a mission. He exudes confidence! It was hard to imagine that this happy, joking, energetic, cordial, friendly fellow was carrying the personal burdens which he proceeded to unload—a case of unresolved grief.

The Story as it Unfolded:

Mr. Clarke stopped one day on his way out of the hospital, and said he would like to talk to me "one of these days, real soon. Could we get together?" I assured him I would have some time, and an early date was set for our conference. This was postponed several times. Then I chanced by his office one day and he invited me in. He began: "I have been wanting to talk to someone about this for a long time. Something you said not long ago prompted me to speak to you that day on the hospital steps; but I really wasn't ready to talk about it, so I put you off. You bothered me when you said you were going to be writing on the subject of grief and that you were conducting a survey among pastors. I knew then that I was going to have to come to face this problem squarely one day. You can see that I have been putting it off by the way I have postponed one appointment after another. I really didn't think it was a problem. I thought I had it neatly tucked away, but it isn't so. Last summer when I was in training at the hospital this kept coming up as the student-pastors began to take a closer look at themselves. I couldn't share this with anyone then, so I just stiff-armed them when they came close to looking at my 'innards.' Not me, I had the world by the tail, and I was hanging on for dear life. Something else you said got me to thinking, too. You said that grief could be delayed for a long time; you cited the case of the woman who had been grieving over her brother for 20 years. I have given that a lot of thought . . . (There was a slight pause, the counselor almost knew the next lines, but he waited.) It happened not long ago; I was putting my daughter to bed and I leaned over to kiss her good night and I said 'Good night——' and I caught myself saying my first wife's name. It really stunned me. Could it be that I had not worked through it? I thought I had. This girl is a 'dead ringer' for her mother . . . (He caught himself.) That's not a pun. But when I look at her I see my first wife as plain as day, to use another old cliché. Funny how that slipped out. . . ." (He saw it clearly for the first time, that he had not been able to blot out the image because he daily lived with a symbol of it incorporated in the child . . . We cited Lindemann's work about effective grief work, which he maintained had to do with just this principle of learning to live with images of the deceased. He had never thought about that, had never heard it expressed that way. He seemed stunned again.) "You mean that I have not been able to get her out of my mind's eye." (I tried to interpret again what Lindemann meant as I understood it. Mr. Clarke said that this began to make some sense now, and then went on to relate some other reminders that he wasn't quite able to get rid of, like two pieces of furniture with which he could not bear to part because they had been given as presents.) "I tried to get rid of the old furniture." He rationalized that it was wearing out anyway. "Then, you know, there's something I have never told anyone. I have my first wife's picture in my dresser drawer, and I catch myself opening that drawer and taking a look at her picture; I do it every day . . . I guess if what you're saying is true I'll have to put the picture away." (I interpreted that some people make the mistake of destroying all the evidence, rather than assimilating the mementos. They make them into memorials and they become shrines to which people repair. He said that that was it, exactly. He went on to say that in all the reading he had done this was the first time that he had heard about this concept of learning to live with images, and he was going to have to think about this some more.)

Another curious parallel arose when he went on to recount how this all began. It was pure chance that the day he had made the

(Freudian) slip about calling his daughter by his wife's name, he had had a funeral of a baby. This he felt was the match that lighted the fuse on his delayed time bomb. He then began to see that there was a chain reaction of events that had toppled the neat defenses that he had built up around him during these intervening years. It all began to fit together. Then he related that his first child had died of an upper respiratory disease shortly after birth. It was accidental; four babies in a nursery died of the same error in judgment of a nurse who unthinkingly had left a window open in the nursery. This was a most difficult time in adjustment, especially, he thought, for his wife whom he had known since childhood. Their first dreams were dashed to pieces on the rocks of disillusionment. That was about where the spontaneous interview ended. We agreed to continue the conversation at a later time.

It was about a week later that many of the real feelings began to emerge in an interview that had been structured to release feelings which the counselor knew were present but had not been mobilized sufficiently. When the interview began, one could notice Mr. Clarke's discomfiture. He obviously knew that he was going to have to face the problem squarely. He admitted that he had been thinking about death a good deal lately. He began by saying: "There is a bit of fear in it, not for me personally but I fear that my family will not be taken care of or that somehow I will not live long enough to make adequate provision. I thought that I had gotten over Muriel's death, but now these nine years later it begins to really trouble me. I blamed myself for her death, and I guess I have been punishing myself for this.

"If we hadn't taken that vacation she might still be alive. I know that is foolish but I can't get it out of my mind. It was my idea to go to this lake. I insisted that we go there and that's what makes it doubly hard.

"Since we talked the last time, this image business has bothered me. I caught myself thinking about it when just reading the newspaper in the backyard, when I was supposedly trying to relax." (This illustrates a principle in pastoral care—that the counselee is often working on the material of the previous interview at those unsuspecting moments when the full force of what has been happening begins to clarify.) He continued: "I was afraid that I might lose that image, and I have been fighting to protect it. I do not think this is a denial of grief. I have been fighting with that concept, too. I know I have to live with it. I know that these children, whom she bore, have to be raised and I have to live with them even if one of them reminds me over and over of my wife. I don't want to lose the memory, and, by God, I'm not going to. Time will not make the memory fade, but it will help to hold the image." (We had talked in the previous interview about Red Skelton and his difficulty in assimilating the loss of his son, who had died of leukemia at an early age, and how Mr. Skelton had not been able quite to "close the lid on the piano," had built a shrine in his home, and had not been able to touch anything in the room that was just as Richard, his son, had left it.) He said he was going to keep the picture in his dresser. "I won't move it; I don't want to move it." (Even though his present wife knows of its existence and they talked about this matter at length both before and after this present marriage, he cannot get beyond this at the moment, and perhaps never will, unless he wants to, or makes a drastic change in his personality orientation.)

Grief, for Mr. Clarke, cannot be seen in an academic sense. He said he found it difficult to be objective *about* or *to* grief. "It is subjective and I can't give these trite answers to anybody, least of all to myself. There is still some resentment. I can't say against whom this resentment is, but it is there. The resentment is felt because I had to go through it. I have a hard time accepting that Romans 8 bit about 'all things work together for good . . .' I could see no earthly good in this and I still can't . . . I try to see some purpose in this action. I guess it's a comfort to know that had she survived she would have been a helpless invalid the rest of her life. I have learned when I am talking with others about grief when to keep quiet, because they can't see any purpose in what has happened to them. I have difficulty separating these things in neat categories. I know I was filled with fear. I didn't know for a certainty that I would ever see her again. I have used this 'In my Father's house are many mansions.' I wasn't sure I believed that this was so. Deep down I believe that Muriel's with God and at peace. I believe in life after death, but I have to struggle to reconcile it in my mind. If only someone could have been through this and come back and told us, it would be easier." (He recognized that there would be no leap of faith.) "I still don't think I lost her entirely.

I went back to the drawer the other day after our talk and there with the picture was a neatly tied little bundle of cards and mementos of the funeral. There was also this card with which I had sent some flowers, on the first anniversary of her death, to the church where we had been married. I was both shocked and pleased to read this message, 'My constant companion still.' That really threw me for a moment. I have decided that I can't throw these things away, and what's more I am not going to . . . Another thing that has become quite clear as we have been talking, and it hit me quite strongly when I went to the doctor for my usual checkup, is . . . (Evidently there has been a bit of preoccupation with his own health) that my first heart attack was on the fifth anniversary of my first wife's death." (He even wonders now if this was a bona-fide heart attack, because he has had no subsequent trouble. He was sitting in the doctor's office and just happened to glance at the chart and the date stuck out like a sore thumb.)

After a brief pause he continued: "It has been difficult to live with the image. I know that when I go to call on people, and I usually go right away, it is easy for me to tell them, 'You don't get over this in a day or the day after tomorrow; nor do you just grin and bear it.' I tell them it will take at least a year to even begin to live with the idea of the loss . . . Another thing I didn't realize I was doing—oh I guess I knew it—but, I would end up sharing my loss with them. I knew then they weren't interested in my grief, but I could scarcely go through a session with a family without in some way letting them know that I had been through it.

"There is one thing that I can't remember much about, and it's strange—that's the funeral. I draw a complete blank. I remember a few snatches of what went on. I have no recollection of picking out the casket or even being in the funeral home. I know my brother sat next to me, but that's only in retrospect. The three men who conducted the service were friends of mine, but I don't remember what was said except one of those silly little things. Well, it isn't so silly. I remember the poem, in part, one of them used, and that's all. It was about sailing ships: 'some are leaving, others are arriving.' It's been the only thing that I have held on to all these years."

The conversation had to end here; the thread has never been picked up again. Perhaps one day it will be. There will be no pushing for it; it will be resumed only when he is ready, and wants to talk about it. The door was left open.

The reader will readily note that this crisis has never been fully and finally resolved. No attempt was made at solving the problem except to let him talk it out. He was quite angry between sessions, knowing not only that he was going to have to talk about it but also that he did not want to lose the image of his wife. The counselor's suggesting his learning to live with the image of his first wife was apparently the "stopper." He wanted to preserve forever and indelibly inscribe the image. He is unwilling at this point, to come to grips any further with it. While he has made a seemingly satisfactory adjustment to his second marriage and there is a great deal of understanding by his second wife, nonetheless Mr. Clarke will not face the issue squarely, though he is able to talk about it without coming to the point of breaking down. The feeling was that though he was letting the counselor into his private world, to a point, he was not going to share all of his real feelings. The constant preoccupation, the going to the drawer to look at the picture of his first wife are a manifestation of unwillingness to close the chapter. It is acceptance, but only to a point. He may never be able to get much beyond this point without further exploration and help. He fights for control; he still sits with the clenched fist. His anger and hostility are reflected in the way he holds himself in and in his measured phrases. He gives the impression of talking with his teeth clenched tightly together. He knows that hanging on to this memory is all that he has, and he is afraid that it is going to fade and he wants that least of all. All the classic signs of unresolved grief are evident here. That it has been delayed this long is not necessarily as bizarre as it may look to the outside observer. Time, with the grief sufferer, may not be and usually is not that relevant. The passage of time does not have that much meaning for those who are acutely troubled. Their time-space perception is somehow distorted and they are able to compress or elongate time and events with seeming ease. While this is more pronounced in the psychotic state, it does have its component characteristics in the neurotic, emotionally disturbed states. We are not suggesting here that Mr. Clarke is not able to function fairly well in his parish situation; he is a great help to many people. He has an unusual degree of sensitivity to the needs of his parishioners. He is able to identify very closely with them. While he may use the situations of the grief sufferer to help himself, he is able to help others because they know what he has been through.

Fortunately, it has not interfered with his effectiveness as a pastor or in his overall relationships. In a brief conversation after these interviews when he said he was glad to share this with others who had been going through this crisis, he mentioned that if it can serve as a help to others he would gladly release the content of these interviews. He said, in effect, it will show that a pastor has been involved in this grief crisis, he himself becoming a grief sufferer, and what's more it had not been easy for him. It is still not easy for him. Then, significantly, he added that he realized that the next step was to begin to live with the image of the deceased, but also to go some steps beyond to more healthful living.

What he is saying is reflected in the second example, which relates to a pastor's wife who had an unresolved grief situation of which she was unaware until it was uncovered in the course of pastoral counseling. It points up the fact that no one is immune from grief, least of all the pastor or his wife. Grief is not something that visits others out there, away from my immediate circle; it is not always happening to someone else, but gets into the very fabric of everyone's existence. It also says that problems may masquerade as something else not recognizable as troublesome.

IDENTIFYING DATA:

Mrs. Greene is a pastor's wife. She is 35 years of age, mother of three girls, and is herself the oldest of three siblings. She taught school and has taken graduate work beyond her B.A. degree. She is knowledgeable, attractive, and meets people, in most situations, as an equal. She had become increasingly irascible, easily hurt and insecure in her relationships, especially with members of the immediate family—and more particularly the in-laws. Mrs. Greene came as a self-referral (after her husband had been in a training program).

PRESENTING PROBLEM:

It was quite an effort for her to come because it was an admission, on her part, that at one time she would have been quite unwilling to make—namely, that a pastor's wife did not exhibit more control of herself or her emotions. She was not able in the first part of the initial session to pin it down to anything very specific. Much data about relationship and family were elicited in the general easy flow of conversation. She had begun to look at herself in the light of her present feelings and the many misgivings she had about herself. She was not reacting with what she considered her normal response, and she was more easily irritated by the slightest confusion or reaction of people to her. She was, in her words, "trying to overhaul [her] mind, trying to find out what is really wrong." It was not just one thing—there were many. "My name is legion."

It wasn't until the first interview was almost over that the two salient facts came parading into full view. She said: "It was last fall that I was pregnant and lost it," and "I never did get over father's death (which occurred four years previously). I never really let go on it. I had had my second miscarriage at the time of my father's death. (She has been pregnant seven times out of the nine years of marriage; four of them have ended in miscarriage.) Then, for the first time, the relationship between the miscarriage and her father's death became apparent. Her rebellion against her in-laws is revealed in the kind of hostility she had for her mother-in-law. She did not get back to talking about father for the next two interviews. One got the feeling that she was testing out this idea, that she was skirting all around the subject, unwilling to tackle it. Then she realized that she could not live her whole life in fear, refusing to examine what was really bothering her. To say that she was shackled to the past would not be overstating the case. The feeling, she said, was akin to having a lid clamped on tight, and she was trying to pry it off.

The thing that brought the matter into the open was a visit to the dentist. She had the feeling she was about to faint in the chair, and she literally shook inside. She didn't faint, but was frightened that she would lose consciousness. This may have some bearing on the fact that, in thinking that she would not return to consciousness, she equated death and fainting. It was also at this time that she had given considerable thought to her father's death and so it was easy for her to draw the parallel between fainting and death. It was related to the fact that the visit to the dentist was on the anniversary of her father's death. She said she remembers wanting to be awake during the delivery of her children, so that she could have conscious control.

This is one thing many patients in hospitals feel—that when they are anesthetized they do not have conscious control.

This has also occurred with Mrs. Greene at times when she has fought off going to sleep. She said she never had this feeling until her father's death—and then the fear of her own death became uppermost.

It was not until the fifth interview that she lost control of herself and began to weep copious tears for nearly fifteen minutes. She had been talking about the kind of security she had with her husband, or the lack of it, and she had said that her father had represented security. When this came under threat, with her husband as provider, she broke down and cried. She realized, at that moment, that these tears were for her father's death. She said: "I held up beautifully during the entire time. The people who came, by the hundreds, to the funeral home all told the same story of what a really wonderful guy he was. He always wanted us to be independent, on our own. He wouldn't have wanted me to cry. It was Mother, however, who always told us to put on the front—not to show feeling. That, coupled with the fact that I had been listening to my husband's sermons on death, led me to believe that I had no right to cry. To cry would have been an admission to myself and others that I really didn't believe this immortality stuff my husband was spouting. . . ." She then began to review the "closeness" she had felt for her father, and how she could "go running home and tell him anything." He was, in her words, "predictable." "I could twist him around my little finger and get most anything I wanted." (It was in the next interview that she came back to the same feeling, as she reviewed her relationship with her father. She seemed eager to talk about it now that it was in the open and the tensions she had been experiencing and the pills she had been taking were drastically reduced. The tender moments that were recalled were of the storybook variety as she began to "idealize" her father to the counselor.) "I was his pride and joy—even though Mother wanted a boy." A fierce kind of competition arose between mother and daughter. "He would come and talk to me and he felt that he could talk to me. Mother resented this because he was treating me as an equal. . . ."

(In the ensuing weeks, as she relived her relation with her father, tears flowed more freely and she began to feel more comfortable as a person. She also became pregnant. Though she had been having many miscarriages and felt a bit uneasy about this one, she began to develop more confidence. Things were going along in fairly good fashion until a parishioner hung himself, and all these feelings which she thought she had worked through in accepting her father's death came rushing back to the forefront. She even wondered if she, too, could take her own life. The thought of death again began to be a preoccupying factor, because at this time came the news that a cousin's two-year-old boy had leukemia. There was a strong identification with her cousin. She began to feel guilty and grateful, wondering what she would do if the roles were reversed. "But I began to realize that I could begin to be myself for the first time. I think I have worked beyond Father's death. I know it's all right to express emotion, and being myself is quite a relief. It gives me a sense of power I had not had before . . . I realize that I never grieved properly for my father, and I know that I was feeling sorry for myself . . . I am a sensitive person and soft-hearted in many ways. I guess underneath it all," she continued, "I hadn't accepted Father's death and this kept coming to the fore every time some event took place which challenged my security."

She began to get introspective as the pregnancy continued and the prospect of a new child began to take some of the edge off the old feelings that had always plagued her. She could even watch a play in which the father had no time for his boy. At one time she would have over-reacted. It amazed her a little to realize that after all this time (six months had elapsed from the time of the first interview) she had such feelings. She turned her attention, then, to resolving her relationship with her mother. She began to realize, further, that having been freed from the bondage to the past relationship with her father she could be a free person in her own right—a free, interacting being. When her father died her world had crumbled, but she never told anyone. These feelings were buried inside and never let out until she began to examine why she was having all these negative reactions in her interpersonal relationships. Having once resolved her feelings, she was able to work through the grief situation with the counselor. Until then, the father's death had stood as a roadblock to her achievement of selfhood. She summed it up: "I didn't holler before when I was hurt . . . I know now that I am not exempt from emotion. I am free to be myself."

As the intervals between visits lengthened and she began to feel that she was going to have a successful pregnancy, there was a decreasing need for help. She felt that she was beginning to know now to what she was reacting and could do a more adequate job in being the kind of free person she wanted to be.

The delay in the reaction, in both cases above, adequately demonstrated that it can have a devastating effect on the grief sufferer, just because he hasn't wanted to come to grips with the effect of the loss. In the latter case, it took, at first, a very subtle turn. It was glossed over by Mrs. Greene, and by her husband who told her that the Christian, and especially the pastor's wife, has "to bear loss with a smile on the face or else you belie your faith." She did not believe this, in the beginning, and it took a long time for her to come to the realization that grief denied outlet will erupt into a more serious form of expression; that it will find an outlet, and when it does, the effect can be much more devastating. Pushing it down, out of awareness, she was almost certain to begin to feel its effect in interpersonal relationships as well as in her own intrapersonal relationship—in the things she felt about herself. The fact that she was able to assimilate the loss into her experience finally gave her a freedom that she had not previously experienced. The fourth child was born as this chapter was being typed.

CHAPTER SIX

GRIEF REACTIONS:

WHEN GRIEF IS SEEN As CRISIS

(A Case of Rejection)

Significant loss in human relationships produces a reaction akin to the kind of grief experienced when a death has occurred. In fact, it is hard to distinguish the difference. Symptoms are closely related and are often described as a grief reaction with the same kind of somatic sensations—numbness, distress in the abdomen, drying of the secretions, palpitation, and loss of appetite. These are the same reactions seen in the grief sufferer who has just learned that his loved one has died. There are the accompanying psychological sensations that are manifest in emotional distress. Most common are the rejection phenomena, the divorce action, the withdrawal from the relationship, the separation from routines that were a familiar way of life, and the sudden cessation of the human interaction of interpersonal relationship. In counseling, this becomes clear. There is often inability to cope with the feelings that have been produced; the other partner is blamed for the break in the relationship. Hostility is manifest when the supposed innocent party has been duped by the partner, especially when the spouse is the last to find out about it.

Divorce or separation seems to be the most common phenomenon in which a close parallel exists with the grief syndrome we have described in Chapter One. The ambivalent character of the grief reaction is present. Alternating feelings of hate and affection are produced when the togetherness is broken and someone else has captured the affection of the spouse. As has been indicated, this can be observed in the loss of tangible things as well—treasures of art, keepsakes, mementos. Any kind of significant loss, where the individual has invested a great deal of himself or of his total life work, time, and energy, can produce many of the same kinds of reactions. Loss of job or status, moving as a result of promotion from one community to another, being placed in a foster home, being remanded to jail, being committed to a state hospital, or the loss of limb or any part of the internal organs of the body, to mention just a few more situations, can be thought of as primary or secondary grief phenomena.

These costs are not seen many times in terms of dollars and cents. No services are conducted because such a loss has occurred. All the paraphernalia accompanying the death of someone who is near and dear to the grief sufferer are absent, but the reaction in many situations may be just as profound and equally devastating. The costs in terms of human life and the scars that are left may be equally difficult to deal with and may, moreover, require more time on the part of the pastor as counselor than is invested in the acute reactions at the time of death.

The case presented in this chapter is an illustration of how a divorce action, not by the counselee but by her parents, erupts in later life as a grief reaction. The word that describes Mrs. Crandel is *rejected*. As will become clear, she has had difficulty all her life accepting the fact that her parents were divorced.

THE CASE OF MRS. CRANDEL—*Identifying data:*

Mrs. Crandel is an attractive, young wife and mother of three pre-school-age boys. She has been married about eight years to a rather passive and dependent husband who prefers to stand on the outside of her problem. Originally she was referred by her pastor to The Pastoral Counseling Center because she wanted to talk over some of the problems she was having with her mother. The first appointment was made to discuss her mother's alcoholism and the effect it was having on the counselee. Basically, she wanted to know what kind of help was available for mother. This interview was on a rather superficial level and no further appointments were made because she was not sure that her mother would accept any kind of help.

It was two weeks later that she called to make an appointment for herself for the purpose of presenting her own problem. As she said:

"The problem isn't mother; I need some help for myself." This was June and for the next nine months there were almost weekly visits to the counselor's office, "to find out about me." There was much material of a very personal nature that surrounded her fears—the fear that she would have a mental breakdown; the fear that her mother would do some harm to one of her children; the fear that she would be rejected by her husband; the fear that she would be "left out"; the fear that she would end up as her mother; and the compulsive need to act out her mother's problem.

The real grief situation did not open up until about the fifth interview, when she began talking about the fact that her parents had been divorced when she was ten years of age. From that time on, she and her younger sister had lived with their mother, and maternal grandparents off and on—whenever their mother had work and they had to be cared for. Her hostility toward her mother is manifest throughout the early interviews because she felt she could not get rid of her mother, who caused her all this hurt. "If Mother were 10,000 miles away, this wouldn't be far enough." She wanted to accept her mother as she really was but she could not get to this point. She wanted to stop the vicious circle of rejection because she felt that on account of her rejection she was doing the same thing with her children.

Little things in her own marriage were magnified out of proportion because of the divorce relationship of her parents, about which she was alternately resentful and overwhelmed. The big fear she had when growing up was a result of having only one parent. She did not want anyone to find this out and would tell fantastic tales to hide this fact. She was overwhelmed because she feared that her marriage was going to turn out the same way—she alternately hated her husband and feared being turned away by him. So, in part, she rejected him and her children before they had an opportunity to reject her. This became clear when she began to realize, after a few months of counseling, that all the time she had wanted girls and she ended up with boys. Therefore, she had to reject little boys; the rejection of her husband was also connected with this.

Rejection by her father was very much a part of the picture. It was mainly from her mother and grandmother that she learned that men were not to be trusted. On the one hand, she feared mother was going to reject her and, on the other, mother did everything to protect her from being hurt by men. This accounted for, in part, her feeling "trapped" in her own marriage. What she felt she really needed was a mother rather than a husband, and this feeling persisted strongly for some time. "I want my mother; I want to be a little girl again." While admitting to play-acting the role of wife and mother, the fear that hounded her most was that she would be a failure in her marriage. This would be the worst possible kind of failure, not only because of the cultural overtones of divorce, which she abhors, but also because of what happened to her parents. Therefore, she wanted her marriage to succeed at all costs. She began to realize that the correction had to come from within her own self.

In the tenth interview she finally brought up her father, point blank. She felt that the reason that he had not been mentioned and may have appeared to play such a small part was more significant than she realized. She began by saying she pitied her father, because "Mother was such a bear cat." She found herself taking his side because "Father acted as if he cared for me." Yet there were ambivalent feelings about her father. "If he thought so much about us, why did he leave us?" (This is akin to the death of a parent.) She had the feeling that she never got very close; she didn't know who he was or what he felt or thought. "Would he treat me so lightly, if he were really trying to be my father and love me?" And then, as if turning a switch, she would turn on the hostility button, and alternately feel hate and strong feeling for him, much the same as the grief sufferer in loss by death may feel toward the person who has died.

She remembered a poignant incident that happened one Christmastime when her father came to the door and left the presents and she accepted them and then closed the door on him. At this point she broke down and wept copious tears. She couldn't remember having wept like this before. These were tears meant for the time when he left. This represents a delayed grief reaction.

She had lost a "love object," and this was not completely realized until in the counseling session she relived some of the incidents and recalled some of the memories and scenes that she rehearsed as she spoke. The delayed reaction packed a terrific wallop. She began the very next interview by saying she realized there was a "terrible want for him." Again, pity and disappointment were present in the kind of feelings she was able to dredge up. This was the way things had always been—her being led to expect things from her father and his failure to show or perform.

She remembered the kind of feelings she had when he was about to marry his third wife. Through alcoholism, he had driven the second wife to a premature grave, as he had driven her mother to the brink of destruction with alcohol. There was a feeling of rejection. Somehow she felt that she had been a part of that failure. Father was a strong, dominant, opinionated person. If she leaned on anyone, it was he. The support, however, was only in her feeling life not actually in her day-to-day relationships.

During this same interview she came to the awareness of the loss of an important person in her life. She also became cognizant of the fact that one can have a grief reaction over the loss of some "loved object," just as when someone dies. She accepted this intellectually. He was gone in terms of being emotionally removed. This explained in part her staying away from strong aggressive men, and led her to the submissive, passive husband she married. It also helped her foist her hostilities off on mother who allowed such a thing to happen. She could let mother "dissolve into nothing" and yet she felt terribly guilty about this. She questioned why these feelings happened now. As a result of going into them at this time, she said she began to feel the release from the numbness of grief to the experience of actually feeling hurt. She summed it up by saying: "It is painful; it hurts."

Mrs. Crandel felt that the real split in the relationship between her mother and father had taken place at the time of her sister's birth, when she was about five years old. From that time on, apparently the relationship deteriorated until it could no longer be tolerated. If her sister had not been born, this might not have taken place. She, therefore, began to resent her sister, and while she admired her for her abilities she still resented her.

Mrs. Crandel's father chose to remain aloof from the relationship with his daughters, though he never had children by the other two marriages. He did not care to see her children, and this really bothered her. When the children were injected into the picture, she developed the insight that the reason she resented her children was because they have a father and she doesn't. So her feeling was one of being reduced to a child wanting affection.

She thought that she had been stalled at an early developmental stage in her love relationships and could never progress beyond to the mature love of husband and wife because she had never resolved the relationship with her father. So, all her life she was looking for satisfactory love relationships with men and searching for an adequate father substitute. She began to see that once this has been satisfactorily resolved and "this grief business is out of my system" she would be better able to handle the relationship to her father. ⨍

It was not long after this discovery about her relationship with her father that she was able to visit him. They got into a long discussion about religion. This produced some more of the pent-up feelings that she had not been able to release until then. Father had always prided himself on his irreligiousness, and would not allow her sister and her to be baptized—a source of tension in the home. This was not accomplished until adult life. When the discussion turned to what this meant to her, and the subsequent feelings were elicited, she practically ran from the counseling session because suddenly she saw the counselor as her father.

In the very next session, she began by saying that she knew who the counselor was. "You are my father, to me. Every time you inject something that is personal, I want to tune you out because I want you to be the accepting father, and I so fear that you will reject me." (Transference feelings.) After this was explored and accepted, she seemed to make much more rapid progress. She could even go on liking her mother, and saw that her attitudes, in part, had fostered her mother's alcoholism. She also began to see her father in his true light. He wasn't as much of a threat to her existence as he had been. "I realize once you expose something like this, it flies."

By the time of the nineteenth interview, the relationship with her father was being explored in depth. She was able to talk more freely about it than at any other time. She consciously had felt the rejection, in all its poignancy, and what could not be accepted as a child. This was held over her during her developmental years. She was reminded of it every time she saw a little girl with her father. She had said, "If Father had died, then he would have been gone from the picture and it would have been easier to accept. Then he wouldn't have been around as a constant reminder of the rejection. It's like having the cake on the table and not being able to touch it." This is a part of the ambivalent feelings that grief sufferers experience in relationship to a loss. Her own feelings of responsibility, for somehow having caused this, were still persistent. She had the feeling: "If there was something I could have done to have prevented this." She had a strong desire as she was growing up that: "I would like to patch the whole thing up." She remembered reaching out in feeble attempts to reconcile her parents, but only in her own mind.

By the twentieth interview she thought she could begin to lengthen the time between appointments, and that she was gaining control of her life. She saw her role more clearly as mother and woman, and not as child dependent on "Daddy." It became more painful to come to the counseling sessions than to face the problem. This was interpreted as a sign of more acceptance on her part of the facts of her existence. She began to be increasingly conscious that this acceptance of the pain of loss was beginning to be easier, because she had worked through a large part of the feelings which had been buried. She also saw that her marriage was not "on the rocks" and that her relationship to her husband, though tenuously maintained, had not been broken. While she and her sister suffered from a fractured relationship, her own children would not have to risk this. The insight that developed was that she did not have to follow compulsively what had happened in her own parents' relationship.

She reported also about the same time that she had begun to look at her children in a different light. She was using the same amount of energy in loving them as she had been in trying to restrict them and punish them. The climate in the home environment was changing to an atmosphere of greater acceptance, primarily because she was being accepted as a person as well as accepting herself as a person.

The lengthening of the intervals between interviews was not accomplished smoothly because she at first interpreted this as a symbol of the rejection, of "being pushed out of the nest." She did not see herself as being free to do this, so weekly visits were once more initiated. It was not until the twenty-seventh interview that she could say, "I can space these out on my own." Even though she felt a bit more dependent, at this time, she was able to visit her father. He did not know that she was coming for counseling. She felt he would have been quite brutal about her going to a counselor, especially one with religious orientation. She now felt that she could talk back to him. A good deal of time had been spent on the matter of grief, and she was able to say that this phase was ended. She felt that she was a far better person for it, even though it was painful. It gave her the feeling that she had conquered her first Mount Everest, and as a result was a more mature mother and wife.

It was during the usual pre-holiday depression that some of the old fears began to haunt her—the fear of mutilation; the fear of not being able to be in control; the fear and the fantasy that she is being watched and that others are plotting against her. She knew that these were ridiculous fears, but they were coupled with those relating to father. Her greatest fear was that her father would take one of her children and either harm him or teach him that there wasn't any God.

The counselor was away part of this period so some of the old moorings had come loose. (This is a calculated risk taken by all counselors when they have extremely dependent counselees.) She was able, however, to invite her father and his present wife to her home for the holidays. This represented a giant step forward. After the counselor's return she was able to investigate some of the deeper feelings she had about the split-up between her father and mother, and she could see the stages of her early development more clearly than before. She thought that a good deal of the trouble resulted from her mother's inhibitions and sexual frigidity, which drove her father from the relationship. She now handled the mother situation much better. Whereas before, a five-minute call on the telephone from her mother would set her off for hours, she now felt she could take her mother or leave her. This also represented a healthy sign of freeing herself from the shackles of the past. The emotional debt to her mother was paid off. All that was left was the mortgage-burning ceremony. She developed further insight about the counseling relationship in which she saw, as she said, that: "You really don't change things; you have to live with them. You are the one who changes." She also saw the counselor as her accepting her father and she was comfortable with this image. He was no longer the "crutch father" on whom she had to lean for support. When she saw the counselor as the good father she saw "a father pushing a child on a swing," and wanted this to be happening to her. This still bothered her a good deal but its pain was less sharply felt.

In the final four interviews much progress was made in consolidating the insights she had gained or was in the process of gaining. Father had come back into her life briefly and had been present for her birthday for the first time in years. This was a real gain as far as she was concerned. The realization that there was a lot of love around just for the asking entered itself upon her consciousness. She was also certain that she had done much of the shoving away of both her parents. There was a new basis for relationship with them because she saw them as individuals who made a decision that adversely affected her life. She could admit that she had been a truly unhappy person because she had had the need to be needed. When she wasn't the center of attention she began to feel sorry for herself and "not wanted for her own sake."

She could come to the counseling hour and announce confidently that the last two interviews would be the *last* two. She said that the emotional freight from the past had been discharged. She could fend for herself. She knew that she wasn't completely "out of the woods." She could continue to come, but she felt that she had to try to stand on her own. Tears welled up in her eyes with the realization that the relationship was at an end, and she slipped silently out of the counselor's office without looking back. The feeling on the part of the counselor was that she had achieved a degree of selfhood and that she had finally faced her life squarely and was able to slip into the future more confidently.

Thirty-five interviews and nine months from the start of counseling, Mrs. Crandel emerged as one of the truly emancipated individuals who had faced the grief crisis of rejection openly and painfully, but nobly, head erect, and with a new sense of being an authentic person in her own right. The fears would still be in the background. She would be able, however, to live comfortably with her past, knowing what she had been through.

The grief problem in this situation was shrouded and covered over with many layers of personality conflict—in her marriage and in her relationship to her children—until she worked through the grief situation of having to give up her father, or having been given up by him. He did not, however, move permanently out of her life. Still she did not possess him in the sense that other children have a parent. When he left, or walked out of her life, she drove her grief into the background so far and so completely that it took considerable time and energy to ferret out the real problem. It is readily conceded that the counselor was not looking for this kind of problem when he first began to work with Mrs. Crandel. It did not begin to emerge until four or five interviews had taken place. The counselor might have been diverted by her unsatisfactory relationship with her husband or the attitude toward her children and mother (both of whom consumed huge blocks of time in the interviews). But the central fact of rejection emerged, time and time again, so that one was led to the conclusion, tentatively, at first, that the grief crisis was the main avenue that had to be pursued. When she was able to invite her father into her home, and subsequently to maintain a relationship with him in spite of what he had done, the turning point in her emotional health was reached.

Mrs. Crandel worked through all the ambivalent feelings of hostility and resentment as well as guilt (that she had caused the break between her father and mother). She had been helpless in the face of the crisis, and had turned in upon herself with self-blame and pity.

Her unwillingness to face the issue squarely provided the excuse to remain dependent, however neurotic were the satisfactions gained in this way. When she began to shoulder responsibility for herself and she emerged from the cocoon or the armor she had thrown defensively around herself, she began to blossom as a person. Though she still had some doubts and fears and anxieties (these are never totally absent anyway), she was able to maintain a healthy balance between things as they were and things as they are now. When she was able to relive the experience of growing up—and growing up in a very unhealthy environment at that—and work through these stages of her development, the chains to the past began successively to fall away. She had to relieve the pressure of being in bondage to the image of her father—pressure she had borne from the moment of crisis when he walked out of her life. This she was able to do successfully because she did not take any short cuts to the relief of her anxieties surrounding the "death" of her father. She thought it would have been easier had he died; the grief would have been worked through easier because this could have been accepted and could have been socially more compatible. She wouldn't have been able to do anything about it if he had died. With the acceptance of the fact of her father's rejection (though never voiced as such), she could then go back and see how this thought had persisted throughout her life, making her an emotional cripple. When she had assimilated this fact in her experience (a stage in the process of grief work), she could arrive at the realization that it was she who had then pushed her father away because she didn't want to face the taunt and ridicule of not having a father to whom she could go or who could "push [her] on the swing," as did other children. This was her ideal concept of the true father in the family. It was more vividly seen when she thought about the counselor, who went home to a family. This family relationship represented the ideal for which she vainly sought in her own existence. There were times when she would tune the counselor out of her immediate association and appear to be wholly detached from the present counseling situation, especially when she was lost in reverie.

Though her mother never left her in the same sense in which her father had, she blamed her mother unmercifully for causing this to happen. This is akin to blaming someone else, like the doctor, for not doing enough to prevent the death of a loved one. She began, in the relationship of counseling, by wanting help for her mother, but ended up seeking help for herself since she was not able to cope with the hostility she felt toward her mother. Neither could she cope with her relationship with her husband and children, who became symbols of the past. They had taken the brunt of her inability to cope with some of the basic facts of her existence. The most basic one was that in her early development she was without a father; he had "died" the day he left the family.

This carried over as emotional freight from the past, which could not be discharged until she was able to work through these experiences with a pastoral counselor who was willing to devote much time and patience to the recital of her past and help her to remove the roadblocks to her becoming a person.

When she finally accepted the loss, assimilated it into her experience, and was able to adjust to the set of givens of the past, she then became the determiner of her health. This was the most significant therapeutic gain in resolving her grief suffering.

The pastoral therapy consisted of listening carefully (with "the third ear") to the recital of the past. The pastoral counselor had to have an awareness of what was going on behind the words that were spoken. He had to be willing to wait her out until she arrived at the insights she needed to assimilate the past into the present. It was a supportive relationship that undergirded her when all other props had suddenly given way. There was a patient, painstaking covering of the areas of her relationship with all the important persons in her existence. Facts and fantasies were separated and clarified; feelings were understood; ambivalences, ambiguities were accepted, and restated. The counselor had to be aware that progress is made slowly, so there could be no pushing for any premature solutions. When we tried to lengthen the time between sessions, she felt rejected and some of the gains were lost. The strong dependency which was built up over the months of counseling was utilized to make her feel acceptance of herself as an individual. When she began to wean herself, the most significant progress took place. When she got to the point at which she said "I can go it alone from here," a new person emerged. The bondage of the past was over; she was able to take a healthy approach to the present and she looked forward to the future to put into effect her new-found freedom as a person in her own right, fully emancipated, no longer a rejected grief sufferer.

It is now several years since this encounter. Mrs. Crandel continues to hold on to the gains she made; she is able to enter into meaningful activities in her Church and community life, and has taken an active part in promoting family life conference for summer camp for the entire family. The rich, rewarding experience she has had with her own children and husband has been put into a constructive channel, and she has a freedom she never experienced before. She is a fully creative person who has worked through her grief crisis in a way that has ennobled her life and has enriched those around her.

CHAPTER SEVEN

The MEANING Of The FUNERAL

Funerals are for the living. Such a bold statement may seem obvious, yet we need to remind ourselves of this basic principle. It kept recurring again and again as this chapter was outlined. The question that naturally follows is: What does the funeral mean to me? I know what it is like; I have been through it several times. I have lost my father, mother, and two brothers. I remember the awful moment of seeing someone I love cold as stone, though cosmetically restored to what he or she looked like. Lifeless clay! It was a chilling experience, like icy fingers up and down one's spine, felt in the marrow of the bone. How much easier if I could have run and hidden and pretended that it was only a fleeting fantasy. It was a subjective experience about which one could hardly be objective, perceived as if one were in a hypnotic transition before sleep. The flood gates of tears were hardly able to be contained. All things meaningful suddenly stood still—the dread, the overwhelming sense of panic, the despair, the hopelessness of the moment, the contemplation of how life would ever have meaning again. I thought, my God how? Why? Why now? My feeble brain could not grasp the significance of the moment. I groped in darkness for direction, but no avenues seemed to open or make sense.

One can afford to be extravagant with words later, but not so when one is feeling lost in the trackless waste where no surcease from emptiness will come. There is no one really to soothe; no one to comfort. The mind rebukes every effort of solace. There is no time to contemplate—only the necessity of swift decisions. There is aloneness, a weariness of thought, a lack of physical energy. Random thoughts run hither and yon—all is meaningless motion.

Russell Dicks dramatically personalized this experience in *And*

83

Peace at the Last[1] by recounting his feelings as he contemplated his own death. It is the kind of exercise in which few will care to engage, but, as Thomas Kepler develops the rest of this book, the main theme that emerges is the necessity for contemplating this phase of existence before it creeps up upon one unexpectedly.

Funerals satisfy a need to be remembered—a need that cannot be met by cold, impersonal memorial services. To be remembered even in death cannot be accomplished by eulogy. The funeral permits a fitting tribute to the end of one phase of existence and the beginning of another. We will soon be "forgotten as a tale that is told," so why not allow the family to make the most of this opportunity? It will stimulate them to face up to the actuality of loss.

I'd like to believe that there would be family and friends who would accord me the dignity of a decent burial. Funerals, for me, emphasize the kind of identification I have tried to establish with other men, that they and I are persons of worth. If I say I believe in the Resurrection of the body, then why is this body suddenly so profane? I do not subscribe to the fact that this "carcass" has no significance. Our Lord was accorded honor and dignity in His death. I don't know what kind of body I may have in the next world; this is the only one I have known, so please don't desecrate it by thinking that it is unimportant or not worthy of consideration.

As I am a Naval Chaplain, it is my privilege to be buried at Arlington National Cemetery with all the pomp and circumstance afforded any of our country's fallen heroes. My wish is to be buried with full military honors, as one who has lived with men who have known how to die for their country. I like pageantry and drama. Let my funeral symbolize the highest and the finest kind of tribute. (Should I deserve less?) Sing the songs of faith. Make it be a witness to the Christ I have served and loved and to the country I have served and loved. Weep, but not for long, for there will be tasks to do, new burdens to bear, new joys to seek and find. I should like to be remembered as a servant of Jesus Christ. Tell others that they too may take up their duties and follow Him.

So when I die, there had better be a funeral. Bury me in the style and the way I have lived. To my funeral director friend, I would say,

---

[1] Russell L. Dicks and Thomas S. Kepler, *And Peace at the Last* (Philadelphia: Westminster Press, 1953).

"Don't charge my widow for any frills, unless of course she says, 'He would have liked that.' And when you take the pastor aside, say to him, 'I don't care how long you take; comfort the sorrowing, speak to their hearts. If they want to display emotion, let them cry, but know for a certainty that I am interested in everything that's done to make sure they grieve properly.'"

When we assert that funerals are for the living we are talking about the highly personal, subjective nature of this experience. With the exception of the Protestant Episcopal Church, the Greek Orthodox, a few Lutherans, and, among the non-Protestants, our Roman Catholic brethren, the main stream of Protestantism would accept the statement that funerals are for the living.

The funeral serves to personalize and to actualize the loss. In the Episcopal tradition the emphasis is on the prayers for the repose of the dead man's soul. Since the emphasis is on the soul of the departed, what the grief sufferer gets is largely the by-product of comfort from the supportiveness of that particular communion of saints. The funeral, nonetheless, becomes a vehicle for the expression of grief. It gives the grief sufferer needed support and the opportunity to vent feelings to those who are most concerned. It provides a channel for expression, an opportunity to render words and gestures of esteem.

Floral tributes are important to the extent of remembering the good deeds of the dead. They give some members of the community opportunity to express by flowers what they cannot express by words. The funeral services are designed with the same purpose in mind—to give formalized expression to one's grief.

1. *Funerals satisfy personal needs.*—Even if the disposition of the dead could be done away with quickly or the trend moved in the direction of quick disposal and hurried cremations, there would still be need to have some kind of ceremony. Death destroys meaningful patterns of living. It is disrupting as well as disturbing to the stability of the family. The personal equation, quite apart from all other consideration, needs to be satisfied. The usual patterns of support have given way. The funeral becomes a means of expressing the sorrow in a direct fashion. The early Christians tore their clothes, physically abused themselves, and donned sackcloth and covered themselves with ashes to personalize their sorrow. They expressed it, further, in tears and wailing. The funeral provided a necessary outlet not only for strong emotion but also for the sharing of the loss. The loss has to be talked out by most before they feel free. The funeral gives the grief sufferer opportunity to vent his feelings in a manner socially acceptable to those who are most concerned. The old family wake served this function by drawing relatives closer as they expressed their loss in each other's presence. As one pastor who was interviewed said when he and his wife experienced the loss of their third child, "We just talked and talked and talked until it was all talked out. We told everybody and anybody and we grew in the process; we became free by talking it out. We also grew closer to each other."

We should not treat the needs of the mourner lightly. They may be unduly sentimental, but no attempt should be made by the pastor to circumvent this expression of grief.

It is an essential concern of the pastoral care of the family that their needs be taken into consideration, not only in the planning of the service but also in the content that the service will have. While a funeral service is an opportunity to evangelize, the simple proclamation of the fact of Christ's conquering of the two great enemies, sin and death, can be the single thrust of the message. It serves as a challenge to the family to accept anew the burdens and blessings of life. It summons friends and community to support the grief sufferers in this, their darkest hour. No pie-in-the-sky, supercilious, sentimental sayings will in any way cover up grim reality. They will simply push the inevitable day of reckoning with the loss that much farther away. When the pastor himself is not able to come to grips with the reality of the situation the sufferer feels that he is not understood and that his loss is being dealt with lightly. The glossing over, the attempt to apply salve which he knows may not be salutary, does a disservice to the family and ultimately to the Church, which, above all else, symbolizes hope—but in the context of reality. The writer once participated in a military funeral for a young father of three who had been killed in an automobile accident. The service was conducted jointly with a civilian pastor who proceeded to recite a poem about a divine junkman who gathered up all the old and the new clocks. This was so completely out of line, in terms of personalizing the death for the young widow and the children, that I could scarcely control my nausea and anger.

A pastor's knowing the personal history of his parishioners and placing himself in the position of recipient of the best in pastoral care and concern would leave little room for ignoring the personal needs of those whom he tries to help understand the mystery and the burden of having to die.

2. The funeral: a vehicle for expression of loss.—The funeral becomes the vehicle for the beginning of the expression of grief. It aids in the process by dealing with the problem of death in a realistic way, although this is not always evident in the way certain services are performed. The funeral provides a climate of mourning and, though some may feel that at times things are a bit overdone, it has a therapeutic significance.

We have said that the grief sufferer needs the funeral in order to speak about his own needs for identification with the deceased. He needs someone and something to hang on to—to remember, to fix forever in his mind this image which will fade. He is confronted with a seemingly impossible situation; he cannot fight back, the chapter is ended, the book is closed! Here is where the pastor earns his spurs. To be able to meet the needs of the grief sufferer is a demanding kind of ministry. That is why it is becoming so important to meet individual demands rather than to conduct services irrespective of personal needs. The grief sufferer expects the pastor to conduct a meaningful service, even though he may not remember much of what is said. The pastor should ask himself the following questions:

1. How am I going to make this meaningful?
2. What would I want someone to say to me if I were enmeshed in the throes of emotional upheaval as a result of loss?
3. What are the needs of these people as I have known them or as they have been expressed to me?

Knowing the grief sufferer's personal history makes it easier to communicate a meaningful and helpful message. Although he may not remember your words, he will remember that you were there in the midst of his sorrow. Perhaps a typed-out copy of the message may be presented on the pastor's first post-funeral call. It may be given as a parting gesture.

3. *The funeral is a learning experience for the survivors, for the community and the Church.*—Every funeral service teaches the survivors, and others on the fringe of this experience of death, the finiteness of man—that he is limited, that he has only a transitory existence. Our days are numbered, mortal flesh must come to an end. It teaches us in the words of the Psalmist "to apply our hearts unto wisdom." "So teach us to number our days." Or, as Saint Paul says, we seek a place beyond this day; here we have no abiding city.

There is nothing so final as death. The funeral service, geared to the living, has as one of its aims to teach that we have a God who cares for us and that belief gives needed strength for any situation that may arise. We walk confidently by faith and not by sight.

The Christian religion emphasizes the worth of each person, and teaches that God does not forsake His children. "I will not leave you comfortless," that is, without strength to bear. Though the grief sufferer can see no purpose in the action of God and may ask the all-inclusive and incomprehensible, *"Why?* Why did this have to happen?" nonetheless he can take a leap of faith, trusting where he cannot see the road ahead. The son of the Commanding Officer of the ill-fated United States Submarine *Thresher* said it best: "God will take care of us."

The Christian religion emphasizes, further, that even though a man dies there is something about him that is deathless. We call it the soul, the very life of God and man.

The Christian religion also is beginning to teach that there are no short cuts to the acceptance of loss. The attempts to delay or deny grief are done with grave peril. Even if there is belief in the deathlessness of man, we still cling to life. We do not want to close the chapter. To the Christian it is the ending of one cycle and the beginning of a new. Part of the mystery that surrounds death is occasioned simply because we do not know what is beyond. The aura of mystery makes us fearful. It is a perfectly natural feeling and should not make one ashamed or feel despair. These themes can be developed by the pastor to make the funeral meaningful.

The Church offers a philosophy of life, a source of strength. It is a resource so real that anxiety ceases to be and one can move out into the stream of life again. The Church offers a redemptive fellowship of concerned people with whom grief sufferers can be themselves. Few there are who find it or understand it!

4. *The funeral provides the community opportunity to express its concern.*—The Church through its members, the fellowship of the concerned, helps by sharing the burden. It eases the load, comforts and lends individual support when the props of life suddenly give way.

Grief sufferers need more than sympathy, although this is necessary. They need empathetic care; someone to stand by in their distress. They need the warmth and companionship of unhurried relationship. They need friends before whom they can cry unashamedly, friends who accept and understand that these are moments of pathos and tragedy. They need friends who do not run from crises, who are aware that there is loneliness and isolation, physical and spiritual fatigue.

Doing things for the bereaved may be a therapeutic help for those closely associated, because it gives them something to do. The core-group in a congregation mentioned in Chapter Four, who have worked through the process of grief, may fulfill some of these important needs for service. Caring for young children, bringing in food, running errands, and standing by to help in any way possible, all make things run more smoothly and help remove some of the stress and strain on the bereaved. This is one way in which Church members can be of valuable help, especially if they have themselves been through the experience and found this service by others to be helpful and comforting. It is a logical and legitimate concern of the caring community. This is especially true if there are few relatives or if the family is widely scattered. Even if the gestures are not accepted, they are often appreciated because it says more loudly than words: *You care!* If the Church is the fellowship of the concerned, here is the place where benevolence can be demonstrated most appropriately.

5. *The funeral is a learning experience for the pastor.*—The funeral is a learning experience for the pastor as well as a service rendered in the name of the Church. The pastor, if he is alert to and aware of human need, will personalize this service so that the grief sufferer knows not only that he is trying to give assurance of life after death but also that he is in the struggle with him. Paul Irion, in *The Funeral and the Mourners*,[2] writes at great length about the personal equation as the real function of the funeral. The essential concern of the pastor is to meet the need of the grief sufferer, individually. The funeral rites are designed to be of help not only for worship but also for meeting the real needs of the people, who are served. The elements of worship and service are paramount. Each time the pastor officiates at a funeral, however, it should be a learning experience for him. It should be no less such an experience for the funeral director.

Upon hearing of the death, before the pastor makes his first contact he should, if he has personal knowledge of the deceased, immediately review in his own mind his previous existing relationship with the person so as to prepare for the visit. He should anticipate something of what he may find when he arrives upon the scene. He should go as a thoroughly open individual so that he may respond to whatever need may be encountered. He should bring whatever resources he can utilize in the situation, whether prayer, Scripture, or just listening. He will come to listen to a recital of events. He may be expected to pray, to offer his services. He will acknowledge that there are practical tasks to be done, and he will go about them in a slow, measured step, responding to needs being expressed. He will remember that he does not stand alone. He will carry the same receptive attitude into the funeral, tailoring his comments and his Biblical and spiritual resources to speak to that particular situation and no other.

Sensitivity is an indispensable quality. It allows one to get beyond subjective reaction to the place where the grief sufferers are. The pastor will have to marshal all of his own strength to be able to minister to their weakness, but he should not ride roughshod over those who grieve with moralizations. This is no time to make the funeral home where he conducts most of his services, into a classroom of theological dogma. The listening ear he has employed before can be turned into a mouthpiece that communicates his understanding of their "slings and arrows." He doesn't have to say anything. The fact

---

[2] Paul E. Irion, *The Funeral and the Mourners* (New York: Abingdon Press, 1954).

that God cares, that ultimately these things are faced and accepted, and that life is a continual life, death, rebirth, and renewal, is communicated because he is there.

Some Pertinent Questions

After the funeral is over, if it has been a learning experience, the pastor should begin asking himself some questions in order not only to evaluate his service but also to determine how he could have achieved a more meaningful relationship or service. These are some of the questions he could ask himself in evaluation of any funeral service he conducts:

1. What was my own reaction to what happened?
2. What did I feel was accomplished?
3. How meaningful was the service I rendered?
4. How were my services received?
5. Did I achieve a feeling of cooperation with the funeral director?
6. Did we really work together in a team relationship?
7. What can we do to be of more help to the grief sufferer when we work together again?
8. What elements in the service would I do differently, if I were to conduct the service over again?
9. What is my relationship to the grief sufferer to be in the post funeral contacts?
10. At what point may I fruitfully begin my pastoral care to the grief sufferer?

The Follow-up Contact

The pre-funeral contact and the funeral itself have therapeutic significance. The follow-up contact between the pastor and the grief sufferer, and usually with the whole family, cannot be discounted. This is also an essential task, separate and distinct from all other pastoral tasks. Most of the work is done beforehand. There is more time afterward that is not hurried by the pressure of a funeral schedule. Several calls may be necessary, especially if he is to get beyond the expected professional, pastoral duties. The pastoral call serves to go beyond the funeral toward putting into effect the bridge relationship he may have talked about, as the Christian community's responsibility to the grief sufferer. It is, in reality, an extension of what was started at the funeral. The two essentials for a therapy for bereavement are (1) "emancipation from the deceased," and (2) "learning to live with the image of the deceased."[3]

There are cathartic opportunities in the post-funeral contact to explore the feelings that need to be discharged. Enough time is allowed for the grief sufferer to gather his thoughts, to find acceptance, and to begin to integrate life at a new level. However, the pastor ought not to push for reintegration too quickly. His very presence will communicate the idea that *someone cares*. Thus, he symbolizes more than he says.

What the pastor is, the attitudes he takes, and how he conducts himself, not only in the interpersonal relationship of the funeral, but also in his understanding of the dynamics of mourning and the individual grief sufferer, may help a great deal with healing, which demands a sensitivity to human needs and a flexible concept of the interpersonal relationship. It further demands a critical appraisal and reappraisal of what the pastor is currently doing in his ministry to the grief sufferer. This will help to sharpen his skill so that he achieves the healing, permissive relationship. This pastoral relationship is what the grief sufferer has to depend on for support. It offers sustaining of values which the individual may have shunted aside during the funeral.

The relationship is the steady anchor which can hold fast during the stormy conditions on the sea of doubt, when no good purpose can be seen. The relationship offers stability, a strength that comes in the interchange of feelings and sadness. The pastoral relationship offers the steadying influence of someone who does not run when the going is roughest. Providing the listening ear may be all that is necessary in order for the healing process to begin.

According to the survey reported in Chapter Nine, most pastors always follow up with a post-funeral contact. Very few are engaged, however, in any sustaining counseling relationship, which seems to be one area that bears further pastoral investigation. The grief sufferer may flounder for some time, and ought to be routinely checked, at regular intervals, through the first year after the funeral. The visits may occur once a week at first, then once a month, gradually length-

---

[3] Erich Lindemann, *op. cit.*

ening to quarterly visits. The critical period will be between the third and the sixth months. The pastor ought to watch for signs and symptoms of inappropriate behavior beyond the usual preoccupation with the image of the deceased—aggressive, hostile attitudes, inactivity or overactivity, and lack of responsiveness to new relationships.

Special Categories Which Demand Attention

It is difficult for most pastors to come to grips with death as a result of suicide. If the deceased was a member of the Church, the pastor may feel that he has not been diligent enough in his pastoral ministry, especially if he has seen the individual in counseling or he has known that the person was a potential suicide. When someone has died by his own hands, the tendency is to treat the family in a different manner than the family whose loss comes through some disease process. The failure to realize that this individual was undoubtedly emotionally or mentally sick may cause the pastor to throw his better sense of judgment to the winds. When pastors are questioned about how they would conduct a funeral of a suicide they say that this would be in a different category. The tendency has been to emphasize judgment and law instead of gospel, forgetting that the essential concern is comfort to the family. The aim of pastoral care is not to remonstrate with the grief sufferer. Its main concern should be to help the grief sufferer begin to rebuild life without the deceased. The pastor may be tempted to take out his own feelings because he was helpless or failed to help in the situation. The grief sufferers, too, may be experiencing some extreme pangs of guilt. The act of suicide seems to announce that the deceased was getting even with them or someone for some imagined or real wrong. Most suicides are suicides of revenge.

The pastor needs to appraise the situation as it is so that he can provide necessary healing balm, rather than rub salt into the wounds. An attempt to uncover the motives and to explore the feelings of the deceased may help the survivors to know that the pastor is willing to enter into meaningful relationship in spite of what has happened.

In an exercise[4] on a Home Examination at the end of the six

---

[4] Readers may want to cover each section before proceeding to the other parts of the outline, write out for themselves what they would do, and compare their responses with the pastor-students.

weeks' Clinical Pastoral Training Program in the hospital where the writer serves as Chaplain, pastor-students were asked to take the hypothetical case of a parishioner who committed suicide and show how they would minister to the family. (Thirty men were involved in the experiment.)

Case Study Of A Suicide

This will be a hypothetical case study. It could have happened to one of the families in your parish. One of your members has shot himself because he was despondent over his health and financial reverses. He had been to see a psychiatrist recently about his emotional turmoil; he had taken to drinking, although it was not serious enough to cause him to seek help for it. (a) How would you minister to this family—a wife and two teen-agers? (b) What kind of funeral service would you conduct? What passages of Scripture might you use? (c) As you reflect on your relationship to this man, what do you feel you might have done as a pastor to have prevented this from happening? The following responses are a composite summation of the pastor-student replies.

(A) *How would you minister to this family?* "I would assume that the wife and teen-agers would be in a state of shock, so I would hurry to them as soon as possible to stand by during the initial stages of shock . . . My hope would be that they might, even then, be able to talk about their feelings . . . I would hope that from my acceptance of their feelings and from my respect for them as individuals they might receive strength for the ordeal of facing up to people . . . My ministry to them would not be hurried; the family would want to work through the reason for the tragedy . . . Guilt and hostility would be there, directed perhaps at the psychiatrist, minister, employer, and community . . . As a pastor, I would hope to be able to help them accept and forgive all who may have been involved, particularly the deceased.

"Many of the dynamics of the grief situation would be present. I see my first task as one of helping them talk about the situation past and present . . . I must strive to enter into their sorrowing . . . I must not refuse to accept any of their feelings . . . The pastor should come to announce the gospel and not the law of God . . . This is no place to talk about the evils of suicide. We do not, cannot know all the reasons, so we must trust the soul of the husband and father into the hands of a loving God . . . The family would need to have the sure confidence of the presence of God. It is not a time to teach or preach, but to love and understand. The pastor should make himself available for counseling, to help this family in their grief work by exploring with them the implications of suicide . . . that it is not an unpardonable sin. This family would also need to find reacceptance in the Church and community and readjust themselves to a world that is morbidly curious about suicides. The visit after the funeral might prove to be the most important, especially if it is evidenced that they are not working through their grief and have not accepted the death of the father . . . I would minister to them as adults. This might be more traumatic to the daughters than to his wife. . . .

"The ministering to the teen-agers might follow the guidelines of explaining that suicide is not a responsible, wilful act. A diseased kidney may function in a way that may end in death; so may a sick mind. This is not a hereditary tendency, and children need not fear that they are doomed to this end. Help them to understand that this is not a rejection of them as children . . . Impress upon them the personal concern, the concern of Christian believers and the comfort and hope of religious faith."

(B) *What kind of funeral service would you conduct? What passages of Scripture might you use?* Of the thirty responses, not a single pastor said that he would do anything other than conduct the straightforward burial service, right out of the book, just as he would for any other person . . . "In the service, I could not blink to the fact of the suicide. While I would not refer to it by name, I think I would be able to face the fact without in any way condoning the man's action. Remorse, yes, but not condemnation . . . I would try to have those in the service sense the fact that this is a corporate sin in which we all have a part . . . We all must have acted toward him in such a manner that he had not felt he could have come to any of us for help . . . The funeral itself would call for recognition of the death of this man and could squelch rumors about 'nasty suicide . . .' The family would have the support and the protection of friends as they experience the funeral process and would have come to grips with the reality of death. I would speak to the living about the dead. The keyword would be simplicity and not starkness. The New Testament passages would carry the theme of salvation through the love of Christ for man."

The survey revealed that most pastors felt that they could conduct such a service either from the Church or from the funeral parlor. Some pastors saw this as perfectly proper since they were ministering to the family and not acting in judgment about the action of the deceased.

Passages of the Scripture run the whole gamut of God's mercy and compassion. Among those recurring most often are passages from John 14:1–6, 25–27; John 11:21–27; John 5:24–29; Romans 8:18–39; 1 Corinthians 15:20–38; 2 Corinthians 4:7–8; 2 Corinthians 5:1–10; Galatians 6:1; 1 Thessalonians 4:13–18; Luke 7:11–17; Psalms 23, 40–103, 130 and 139. Most interesting of all was the inclusion of the Old Testament account of Saul's suicide. "The battle went sore against him." The pastor said this seemed to fit the situation. "How human it is to be overwhelmed at this point."

(C) *As you reflect on your relationship to this man, what do you feel you might have done as a pastor to have prevented this from happening?* It is obviously misdiagnosis. All felt that the pastor was not aware of the full nature of the problem. "Routine pastoral calling might have alerted me to the problem in its nascent stages or at least created a better rapport with which to counsel with the man when the problems became more acute. Psychiatric treatment and the problem of alcohol ought to have alerted me to a human crying out for help. The first step in preventing suicide is establishing a personal relationship of trust and confidence. If that did not exist, I could not stop it; if it did and I suspected such action I would have tried to have the man hospitalized for his own protection and treatment. I would not try to deal with the possibility of suicide. The atmosphere would need to be permissive enough so that whatever the problem was, it could be faced and possible solutions arrived at . . . I need to raise the questions: Did I make myself available to the man? Did I know enough about his personal history? Was I sensitive to human need in my calling? Did my preaching have enough pastoral insight to allow individuals to come to me in time of stress? Did I have close personal contact? Building one's sensitivities to human need is prerequisite in any helping situation. Entering into a relationship in meaningful ways may have made this funeral unnecessary, and no one can argue with that."

It is curious to note that not one pastor suggested that perhaps this service could have been a private affair for immediate family and close friends. This might permit a more personalized ministry and spare the grief sufferer from having to contend with those on the fringes of friendship who would be more curious than consoling. This would be true especially if the method of suicide were of a violent nature, such as shooting oneself or any other kind of self-evident mutilation.

Special Need: When A Child Dies

The death of a child is a tragic and traumatic event. We feel the same way about any young person's death because it appears that so much is wasted. Its unbearable character is a result of the utter helplessness in the face of loss. It signifies that the potentials for growth and future are forever cut off. There is the awful sting of death. This is especially true if the child is killed in a terrible accident.

In the depth interviews reported in Chapter Nine, one parish pastor recalled the sudden numbness when told by the doctor that his child was not going to get well. The pastor said, in part, "In the death of an aged parent there is not the same element of grief as there is in other situations." The most tragic thing, in the death of a child, is the climactic nature of the event. "Our only son lived two days. I wanted to hit somebody. Even when people were trying to be kind I couldn't stand this . . . the things they will say: 'God wanted the child in Heaven.' I could only say that your kind of God is my devil . . . That's the way it struck me. The more potential, the greater the degree of intensity. I learned that Christian faith doesn't keep you from pain. It helps you come through . . . There is still frustration in the death of a child or a young person. The situation is more real to me now than the grief for my father, who died just a short while ago. This child died twenty-three years ago . . . I don't think of it often anymore, maybe once a month, but when I think of it, it is as real as when it happened, and it comes back in moments when I am least aware of it."

The incomprehensible "why?" is asked repeatedly, especially when a child is involved. Words are empty. Those who can't accept will not be ready for counseling for some time. These are the grief sufferers you have to bear with and wait out. As one pastor said: "They respond to symbolic action, the things that have meaning for them. Pray, if it seems appropriate, but more and more I am not trying to do anything. Just being there shows that they matter. The real support comes later and will be appreciated if you were there from the beginning."

What he is saying is that there is no substitute for the pastor who stands in the midst of the crisis as a solid ground, while the ground surrounding the grief sufferer is giving way. The pastor becomes an anchor, steady through the storm. More than reading from the New Testament passages such seemingly comforting things as "Suffer the little children . . . ," the pastor ought to be a walking New Testament, communicating that "earth has no sorrow that Heaven cannot heal." The major thing the Church has to offer is firsthand relationship to God. If this is genuine, you don't receive it by talking about it; nobody can give it. This is not just a philosophy; this is a dynamic. Death is one experience, but there is a continuity between death and life.

Cost And Caskets

In this final section we shall speak briefly about cost and caskets. Too often this becomes a dilemma in which pastors become involved when having to conduct a funeral that they feel is costing the parishioner too much money. This problem ought to be laid to rest quickly and finally. The truth is that funerals do cost money, just like all other services rendered. Since we live in a highly mobile society, values and economic stability are constantly threatened. Everything is tied to a cost-of-living index. Funerals and funeral directors have been lampooned about "the high cost of dying." This is, in reality, a decoy to take the focus off the fact that most persons cling to life. This business of dying is faced only when funeral arrangements have to be made.

The natural attack is at this point. Why does this business cost so heavily sometimes? Nobody else wants to do this dirty work and the funeral director comes in as the whipping boy. Whenever the clergy and funeral directors get together, invariably the discussion gets around to costs and more specifically to fees paid by funeral directors to clergy as a part of the bill charged to the family. What most clergy do not realize is that this is all carefully explained by the funeral director when he plans for a funeral with the family. Of course, there are unscrupulous people in every profession. The over-all impression, from surveys conducted by Robert L. Fulton,[5] indicate that most people are not aware what a funeral costs locally, in their state, or nationally. The feeling is that it is a lot higher than it ought to be. When asked what they considered a reasonable cost for a funeral, most of the respondents reported $500 to $900. The national statistic is approximately $850, with a profit of approximately $85 after overhead, and a reasonable salary for management.

It is this writer's conviction that the emphasis is being put in the wrong place. Pastors and funeral directors will have to get beyond caskets and consciousness of costs, realizing that it will cost the living. It is not a matter of high- or low-cost funerals, but rather of the right kind of funeral to serve the needs of the grief sufferer with whom both funeral director and pastor have the privilege of working in one of the most highly charged crises encountered anywhere.

As we contend in the chapter that follows, clergy and funeral directors will either walk together or they will walk separately. The end result will be help, proportionate to their ability, to effect a cooperative venture, or failure.

---

[5] "The Sacred and the Secular," National Funeral Directors Association, 1963. See also Fulton Survey: "Attitudes of Clergymen Toward Funerals and Funeral Directors in the United States." The findings of a survey conducted by Dr. Robert L. Fulton for the National Funeral Directors Association of the United States, Incorporated, and presented by Dr. Fulton at the 1959 N.F.D.A. Convention in St. Louis, Missouri, on October 20.

CHAPTER EIGHT

The PASTOR And FUNERAL DIRECTOR:

A COOPERATIVE VENTURE

To meet the challenge of a closer relationship between the funeral director and the clergyman a series of meetings around the theme "A Program of Sharing" has emerged. Let me describe the program in general and then give you the specifics as developed in the Buffalo Pilot Project.

As early as 1960 funeral service recognized the need for a clearer understanding of the meaning of the funeral, and a discussion of the respective role of the clergyman and the funeral director as together they served the family in bereavement. The first formalization of such a program developed in Minnesota where a series of 12 meetings was organized and conducted in the early months of 1960.

The program was so immediately successful that the National Funeral Directors Association sponsored a project to develop and formulate a plan of procedure to be used throughout the United States. The immediate recognition of the value of the program was such that the demand for guidance and assistance in arranging joint meetings caused the National Association, in 1962, to retain a Consultant in Clergy Relations. The services of this Consultant as of December 1, 1963, have been used in conducting 48 seminars, attended by 6,793 clergymen and 1,897 funeral directors. These have been sponsored by 1,413 funeral homes. Two of the meetings have been with seminary faculties, representing the seminaries in California (1961) and New York (1963). Twenty-seven denominations have been represented including representatives of 24 Protestant churches, in addition to clergymen from the Greek Orthodox, Jewish and Roman Catholic churches. As of this date similar seminars are scheduled to take place during 1964. If one is sponsored in your community, your attendance and participation would be well worth your time.

The format at each meeting calls for presentations by eminently qualified speakers, an open discussion period for questions and answers and the distribution of valuable and informative literature on the subjects of death, funerals and bereavement.

Funeral service is sincere in its desire to meet the challenge for a clearer understanding of its relationship to the clergy. The Buffalo Pilot Project, described at the end of this chapter, is an effective demonstration of the type of program which can be studied and adapted in the area where you live and work.

There has never been a man whom I could dislike, when I really got to know him. This is axiomatic for any beginning relationship. It permits the kind of openness required for a continuing relationship. More and more I am convinced that working relationships between pastors and funeral directors are long overdue. We work together from practical necessity. We are not expected to enjoy this relationship. It has been, all too often, a very formal and awkward encounter. We have not always known how to work together. We have not always talked together, nor have we always wanted to talk together. We have sometimes preferred to make snide remarks; we have attempted to make a joke of a most significant relationship with people.

There is a need for more dialogue if grief sufferers are to be served adequately. Dialogue is communication characterized by hearing what the other fellow is saying and receptivity to it. It is the lack of communication between the two groups that has been the cause of much of the tension. Reuel L. Howe makes this assertion: "Every man is a potential adversary, even those we love. Only through dialogue are we saved from this enmity toward one another."[1]

It is only as both pastor and funeral director run the risk of relationship, through dialogue and working together, that the lives of many people will be affected positively. How we understand one another is through a knowing that is born out of cultivation of the soil of experience. Neither pastor nor funeral director need feel

---

[1] Reuel L. Howe, *The Miracle of Dialogue* (Greenwich, Conn.: The Seabury Press, Inc., 1963), p. 3.

depreciated because he initiates action that moves toward significant relationship. Convictions do not fly out the window just because we do not think alike or have the same point of view or point of viewing. When the other person's thoughts and feelings are known, we begin to appreciate his person and the frame of reference out of which he speaks.

Five structural assertions about this cooperative venture form the body of this chapter and set the guidelines for the areas of further exploration.

I. There Is A Need And Desire For Better Communication Between Funeral Directors And Pastors

Communication happens because people make it happen, and because people desire dialogue. Unless there is mutual desire for relationship, the muddy waters get muddier. The pastor should recognize that he cannot operate in a vacuum. Working relationships go begging either for want of having been tried or because results have not always been satisfying. Just as a wag once said: "Christianity is a good idea; too bad it hasn't been tried." Relationships have a way of remaining on the polite superficial level, at times— saccharine sweet but never coming to grips with the essential concerns. The basic reason for this is that the pastor and funeral director do not know each other and they operate at different educational, social, and economic levels. As we discovered in the survey, they rarely see each other except on their way to and from the cemetery— if they happen to ride in the same car.

We have been through the eras of suspicion and apprehension. Pastors and funeral directors ought to see what is to be done and take some first steps toward a cooperative venture. The best way would be to examine the barriers to communication, and then do something constructive about them in the only place that counts—in one's own community. Where cooperative ventures have been tried, in most instances, the results have not been disappointing, and the benefit has accrued to the families served and the community at large.

It has been argued that the pastor is too busy, or that this would involve another meeting and he has every night scheduled. It can be stated unequivocally that if pastors and funeral directors are too busy to talk to each other they are busier than God intended them to be.

The need to open the channels of communication also exists in the Church. The *dialogue* has not taken place to any significant degree. Reuel Howe, in the work cited above, argues that the reason barriers exist is that the Church has been engaged in a monologue and not in dialogue. He has put his finger on the very core of the problem.

The language barrier. The first roadblock to dialogue between pastors and funeral directors can be simply stated: We do not speak on the same wave length; it is easy to tune out the other fellow. While the average funeral director has heard the burial service and the pastor droning innumerable times, on very few occasions does he really understand what the funeral is trying to say to a particular family. He may know the pastor's style of service so well that he can almost time the funeral by what he has heard the pastor say often before. The theological jargon has been pretty standard, and the investment of words with specific meanings has often robbed individuals of deeper meaning because they were listening but not hearing.

Good conversation is almost a lost art. We are speaking not only of the language of the burial service and what is heard in the funeral parlor or the Church, but also of the kind of conversation that establishes relationships among people. An unexpected visit by the pastor to the neighborhood funeral establishment might be an exciting and stimulating experience. Such initiative is essential to establishing rapport. It will accomplish far more than local ministerial association resolutions. If the pastor bothers to find out what the funeral director is like and what he thinks, he might find him to be a kind, warm, and friendly person who needs to think of the pastor as an ally. Visiting him in his place of business further points up—more than just flattery—a genuine interest and concern for the man personally. If the pastor is going to work with the funeral director, he has an obligation to understand his actions, the language he uses, and what these mean. It is true that in the large metropolitan areas this may be virtually impossible; local conditions would necessarily dictate the feasibility of the suggestion.

In asking funeral directors what the funeral means to them, the writer was surprised to find that it is more than a business venture; it is a genuine concern for people and a need to find some creative fulfillment in doing a task as capably as possible. Visiting might enable the pastor to discover this fact and open the road for better communication.

Prejudicial thinking. The second roadblock to dialogue is prejudicial thinking—the making up of one's mind in advance of actual encounter, or generalizing based on a particular incident. "He's money-hungry," "He caters to Roman Catholics," and "He's more interested in showing off the dead," all have their connotations and speak volumes about the accuser. The image either the pastor or the funeral director may have of the other tends to color the relationship, especially if either lives up to the image which the other has of him. This image may be completely unfounded—merely an inherited prejudice.

No doubt much distortion occurs because of the kind of imagery built up over the years by what the pastor is and what he essentially portrays. The funeral director may have some preconceived notions as to what the officiating pastor ought to be, and he may thus create an image that is out of keeping with the pastor's true character. It is often caricatured.

Since both are important to each other's operation, some of these images are in need of changing. Open and honest confrontation, in friendly atmosphere, can tear the idols down and build new mutual appreciation. Instead of adopting defensive postures, they most need a kind of dialogue that will permit these prejudices to be exposed and these silly myths explored and exploded. When we find out "what makes the critter tick" we are less inclined to be hypercritical. Wanting to meet and talk is taking the other fellow seriously, and it promotes understanding and respect for an individual as a person. It can be a highly important learning experience and one that will redound to the benefit of the grief sufferer whom both aspire to serve.

It is when pastors and funeral directors have known each other that the quality of the relationship shows. While there are individual reactions to individual funeral directors and pastors, on the whole there is much genuine mutual appreciation as persons. If this latter statement is true then the second structural assertion needs further implementation.

II. There Is A Need And Desire To Demonstrate Respective Callings

The word *vocation* is a more descriptive word than profession. *Vocation* is something one is called to do. *Profession* is what one says about his vocation—the way his calling is performed. There is no hierarchy of calling. Each man is called under God's forgiveness. Vocation is not only a calling out; it is a calling to account for what we do with the time we are allotted on this planet. There is no such thing as "universal competence" in any vocation. There are always one- and two- and five-talented men. How they use their respective talents is the hallmark of their competence. There are in every group those who demean and discredit the group as a whole.

One has to be proud, interested, and properly motivated to work beyond his tasks or work will be drudgery instead of fulfillment. It is essential for the pastor and the funeral director not only to know each other and work cooperatively, but also to support each other vocationally. It is distressing to hear pastors speaking disparagingly from the pulpit, or from any other place for that matter, about another man's vocation. They have been too ready to label the funeral director as "money-mad," "profit-hungry," or "making more money than anyone else." It would be unthinkable to stand in the pulpit and say to the floral associations: "Don't charge so much for floral displays," or to the jewelers: "Don't charge such a high percentage of markup," or to the hardware man or grocery man or anyone else: "You have no right to make that much profit." Too often pastors have seen dollar signs in the eyes of some funeral directors and have aired the view that somehow money and funerals are tied up in some unholy way. Neither should the funeral director stand in his stained-glass establishment nor the pastor in his and throw rocks at each other's property. A lot of broken glass will have to be picked up.

Again, all of this stems from a lack of proper understanding of a man's vocation. The only way that anyone can fulfill the meaning and purpose of his life is to render service. As a sage once said, "Service is the room rent you pay for the space you occupy on earth." Each man is called to perform at the top level of his potential and capacity, no matter what the task. Neither pastor nor funeral director should forget that the ultimate aim is to render service to the grief sufferer in a particularly critical situation in life. Their respective services cannot be separated into neat little categories.

While funeral directors may know the general background of the training of pastors, they are often unaware of the theological differences or the fundamental beliefs of one group as opposed to another. The variations within denominations and in seminaries of the same denomination present a confusing picture to the average funeral director. He is relatively certain of what the Roman Catholic position is with regard to the place of the funeral and the usual times the masses are said. With the exception of most Episcopalians, where the local bishop has prescribed some of the customs, and a few Lutherans who insist on Church funerals, the average funeral director is not always prepared for the wide variation of requests that come from Protestant pastors as a whole unless he has worked closely with a particular pastor, in which case he grows accustomed to a given procedure. Little has been done by way of enlightenment either by the pastor or the funeral director. Few have bothered to find out where each other is, theologically speaking. Few have studied the psychology of grief work so as to be abreast of some of the fundamental factors in the grief process that are taking place in most funeral establishments when a service is held there.

Some of the tension between funeral directors and pastors exists because their educational goals and attainments are not the same. The cleavage between being a businessman and a professional man has not been satisfactorily resolved. This rift often causes funeral directors to feel that they have "more on the ball" than the pastor. The clergyman has often felt the same way and has not gone by to get acquainted, just to visit the funeral directors with whom he works or, if he is new to the community, those with whom he will work. It is often observed that though the clergyman may have more schooling this is no criterion for judgment. It might be a good idea for the pastor to find out the vocational requirements of the funeral director, where the schools of mortuary science are and what they are now teaching. While only two years beyond the high school diploma are required in some states, an apprenticeship system is a part of the on-the-job training. The requirements will become more stringent as the funeral directors begin to require more education to obtain licenses. Business practices will begin to sharpen as these requirements become more standardized. The funeral directors do a commendable job in their requirement of high business ethics and, in most states, they do a good job of policing their own group to prevent gouging and high-pressure tactics from becoming a norm of operation.

III. There Is A Need And Desire For Education On The Part Of The Pastor And The Funeral Director

Pastors and funeral directors need to educate each other about their respective roles. First and foremost is the monumental task of educating clergy and funeral directors regarding the psychology of grief. This may be thought an abstraction when through callousness or indifference the whole matter is seen in terms of services—improved and chargeable services. Yet this matter of grief is a very fundamental underlying factor in dealing with people who are in a very critical period. The funeral plays a major role in the grief process. If grief is like a surgical wound that needs to heal, both funeral directors and pastors need to be aware that the funeral is a part of the healing process. From a psychological point of view it helps the grief sufferer to facilitate the grief work and to accept the reality of death. The shattering effect of this crisis results in psychological confusion, and the funeral serves to focus the event and put it into a larger context. As Dr. Clemens Benda said in "Bereavement and Grief Work," "The attempt to make the funeral as inconspicuous as possible is not in accordance with psychological experience. Even if the funeral gives pain to the mourner and causes the outbreak of acute reactions this is much better from a psychological point of view than the neglect of its actuality."[2]

---

[2] Reprinted in *Journal of Pastoral Care*, Spring 1962, p. 10.

Pastors and funeral directors need to understand that they belong to the "caretaking group," to use a phrase coined by Lindemann when he addressed the national meeting of the Funeral Directors in Denver in 1960. They are on the front line of the grief sufferer's experience. How well prepared they are to handle the grief crisis may be due in no small part to how they perform together. Both have the opportunity and responsibility of so performing their functions that the family will be helped in their hour of crisis and that they may have this added strength of being thoroughly understood. The best people are the ones most actively concerned. It is not a matter of putting on a good show or of vieing for the limelight, but rather of attempting to individualize this experience for the family, where, in actuality, the whole matter rests.

The funeral needs to be thoroughly understood with respect to each individual grief sufferer. The pastor and funeral director need to learn from each other what each has to say and do and what each has learned from his dealing with the bereaved. Since funeral directors are involved in more funerals than any one clergyman in the community, such exchanges could prove valuable.

Information is now plentifully available regarding how to better understand the whole psychology of grief as it relates to the funeral, because the funeral directors have become more than interested in this topic. They have become concerned about their roles in relation to the pastor and the grief sufferer. The number of surveys done, at the request of the National Funeral Directors Association, by Dr. Robert L. Fulton[3] points up the attitude of the American public toward death, the funeral, and grief. Most of the recent journals in funeral directing contain articles by both pastors and others with professional concern presenting attempts at understanding and newer approaches to the funeral.

This is necessary not only for the survival of the trade but also for a genuine opportunity to do more than is required by the burial and sanitary codes. This goes beyond cost, caskets, and cremation, limousines for clergy, funeral fees, flowers, newspaper notices, obituaries—important as these practical things may be. This is not a "hard sell" or a "soft sell" job, but a realistic facing up to the fact

---

[3] "The Sacred and the Secular," National Funeral Directors Association, 1963.

that both pastors and funeral directors are dealing with a potentially critical and even dangerous situation. Unresolved grief, like unconfessed sin, can take its toll in terms of human personality; it can limit the free function of an individual in a culture that puts a premium on being free.

More reading must be done, not only about the psychology of grief but also about what is happening in this field. Both before and since the Buffalo Pilot Project, described in a later section of this chapter, conferences have been held, in some places on an interfaith basis, between pastors and funeral directors. Grief psychology has been taught and interpersonal relationships sought.

The most recent books on the subject that were listed in the questionnaire (See Chapter Nine) have not been read by a very large percentage of pastors. There are other equally good monographs by such clergy as William Clyde Donald, III, and Dr. Granger Westberg. The reading of books and the attending of conferences will not in themselves promote better relationships, but reading helps to clarify what should be done to improve one's ministry to the grief sufferer.

If *all* the pastors and *all* the funeral directors were to read even a portion of the information available, some of the concepts and ideas that are being stated could be more easily implemented. This would promote better understanding and would form the common basis for future area-wide and community-wide discussion between pastors and funeral directors.

IV. *There Is A Need And Desire For Interpretation*

The grand old days of funeral directing and the grand old days of the ministry are as outmoded as the Model T Ford. It is an overriding concern, at this moment in the history of funeral directing, that there be a cooperative venture between pastors and funeral directors. Some interpretation of their respective roles is due, not only each to the other but also to the people who are served.

How can the grief sufferer be helped in working through the loss of a loved one or a not-so-loved one—the hostility, the guilt, the resentments, the bitterness, the loneliness? Funeral directors may not have to concern themselves with these things, as a general rule. They need to be aware, however, that such a process begins and is going on in their establishments. Pastors also need to be concerned about these things or there will be delayed grief reactions, denied grief, short-circuited grief, and embitterment. No one expects the funeral director to be a professional counselor, but he can be a good listener. This, too, is a primary requisite for all pastors. If no harm is done, 90 percent of all grief sufferers will be helped.

The desire and need for interpretation comes about because much misunderstanding still exists, not among all clergy but among enough clergy so that the trend toward the memorial service is stronger than many may realize. In the writer's study, the majority of pastors still favor the funeral as such, presently conducted with the American funeral director.

The writer's contention is that the funeral service is a joint venture, though there are pros and cons at this point. A family has arranged for a service. Hopefully, this planning takes the clergyman into consideration. The family asks for the pastor's help rather than his concurrence in such arrangements. One of the complaints of most clergymen is that they have not always been consulted until most of the plans are finalized. There is the matter of fitting the funeral into his schedule, which may not always be convenient or possible.

Part of the ministry of pastoral care is the burial of the dead. It isn't that the funeral director needs a pastor to conduct a service any more than the pastor needs the funeral director. They need each other. Since approximately 50 percent of all Protestant burials are nonaffiliated persons (that is, those who have no church connection at the time of death), the emphasis is not necessarily on the ceremony of the Church. Without this pastoral service, however, it would be a rather austere affair.

Funeral directors need to interpret the belief that quick funerals and cheap burials are not the answer, but that the grief sufferer needs an adequate period of mourning, and that the funeral is an adequate vehicle through which to begin to express this grief no matter how expensive the funeral. Those who have been engaged in formal pastoral counseling centers are aware of the problems encountered by grief sufferers who have not mourned properly—that is, who have not worked through their grief in such a way that they are relatively free persons. This is so principally because they couldn't or didn't know how, and no one helped them by his attitude or action. Grief sufferers in fact may have been hindered by trying to mask or deny their grief by putting on a bold front. Emotion is a part of grief, and to deny expression of it is to short-circuit the process.

Funeral directors are under obligation to interpret the services they offer to people in the community and to the clergy, and there is sound reasoning behind it. This is culturally demanded because we have always buried our dead with distinction and dignity. Funeral directors do not have to apologize for their services and, even though certain attitudes prevail, the only way misunderstanding can be cleared up is to exhibit an openness that leaves nothing to chance or criticism.

The pastor ought also to interpret his role to his people well in advance of the funeral so that they can look constructively at the whole matter before they are faced with funeral planning. One Episcopal rector in the survey had a printed form that was definite in its insistence on a church funeral—that is, "for members only." It was positive, forthright, and was being "sold" to the members. It was an honest attempt to state guidelines for the membership. There can be no quarrel with this if good judgment is exercised and each profession knows where it stands. Part of the resultant confusion is that there are so many variations and no one can predict with any degree of certainty what will meet the needs of the grief sufferer. What may work out well for one individual does not meet the needs of another. Even if pastoral "white papers" or guidelines are prepared, individual differences need to be respected. If both clergy and funeral directors assure the people that they are willing to work with them in providing the most meaningful service and the best in pastoral care to help them as grief sufferers, the walls of suspicion and apprehension will come tumbling down. The kind of image that both pastor and funeral director want will be the kind of image that will be created in the public eye. Imagination is required in funeral directing and the ministry if each is to provide the kind of service most needed and desired by the grief sufferer.

V. There Is A Desire And Need For Implementation

How then do we work with each other? If it is axiomatic that both funeral directors and pastors have to know their culture, the kind of people they are serving, as well as each other, the following is a code of consideration which could help furnish guidelines for launching this cooperative venture:

CODE OF CONSIDERATION

1. Discover the best ways of getting to know one another.
2. Find out what each is doing, thinking, feeling, and reacting in specific situations.
3. Meet together in small or larger groups, from an entire area, from a community, or within a neighborhood (where feasible).
4. Engage in fruitful conversations with the aim of finding ways in which to better minister to grief sufferers.
5. Educate each other about respective vocational roles.
6. Establish a grievance committee (which could be set up with the local Ministerial Association, Council of Churches, and local Funeral Directors' Association) to consider gripes and complaints.
7. Get together on a personal basis to evaluate the last funeral to discover better ways of working more cooperatively.
8. Plan an area meeting (such as the Buffalo Pilot Project) on an interfaith basis, if practical, and invite an outstanding national figure, such as a well-qualified and interested psychiatrist or pastor, who can communicate well to both groups.
9. Follow the larger meeting with smaller neighborhood or denominational meetings, in which such subjects as "The Meaning of Grief," "A Therapy for Bereavement," or "Costs, Caskets, and Cremation" are on the agenda.
10. Engage a lecturer or discussion leader, from those qualified by national reputation, to come into the community to meet on a regular basis. This was done in the Kokomo Project, reported by Dr. Granger Westberg in *Minister and Doctor Meet*.[4]
11. Have a monthly or quarterly luncheon. Put a book or case study on the agenda. Or conduct a group dynamics session with no particular agenda except to get to know each other better and to become more knowledgeable.

---

[4] Granger Westberg, *Minister and Doctor Meet* (New York: Harper & Row, Publishers, 1961).

12. Plan to visit a funeral establishment, to get behind the scenes. While some state laws may prevent observing embalming, where possible make such observations. (The same kind of thing is done in clinical training where students observe surgery or autopsy. The feeling is that they are better able to identify with the surgical patient and/or a family that is resistive to the consent for autopsy.)
13. Do some reading to stimulate thinking and further action.
14. Treat each other as persons. In so doing, the greatest discovery will be made: each bleeds when scratched and yells when hit. Both are human, struggling with doubts and confusions and tensions not only with others but also in themselves.

Pastoral Complaints

In what respect do pastors complain about funeral directors most? The following representative sample is indicative. This would represent approximately 20 percent of all respondents to the questionnaire study. These need to be studied for their validity and comprehensiveness. While they may represent the complaint of a minority, there is the growing conviction that these things have occurred with such regularity, in some locales, as to bear investigation and concern.

1. Costs—overpricing the merchandise and/or services rendered. (*Antidote*: This should be of no concern to the pastor. It is a private affair between funeral director and family.)

2. Planning funerals without consultation of the pastor, other than to get his concurrence as to the time of the funeral; especially, setting the time before calling. (*Antidote*: Make it a rule of thumb to do nothing until consultation can take place between the funeral director and clergy, preferably in face-to-face relationships.)

3. Producing an artificial reality by creating an illusion of lifelikeness. (*Antidote*: Let the funeral director refrain from saying: "We work hard to make him look natural." Just accept what compliments there are and let it go at that.)

4. Emphasizing the body, and the insistence on the open casket. (*Antidote*: Open or closed caskets are really not an issue. Concentrate on having the family present.)

5. Giving the impression that the pastor is working for him or for a fee, or including on the bill the charge for the pastor's services. (*Antidote:* Abolish all fees, except in the case of non-church members. Another possibility is to let the family take care of it themselves.)

6. Competing for holding services in a funeral home. The service from a funeral chapel suggests another kind of competition with the Church. While most pastors favor church funerals, and some, like Episcopalians and some Lutherans, insist on this, by and large the matter has gone by default. (*Antidote:* Have the service from the Church or bring the Church to the service.)

7. Misunderstanding the intent of the funeral as a pastoral service and attempting to combine nonreligious with religious service. (*Antidote:* Let it be clear that it is an act of pastoral care; therefore, hold other services at a different time, apart from the religious ceremony.)

8. Overdoing the decor a bit to the extent of creating an ostentatious and unreal atmosphere. (*Antidote:* Modest, tasteful, non-ostentatious design, and simplicity in architecture will overcome a multitude of criticism.)

9. Piped-in, sentimental organ music and an absence of the great hymns of the Church. (*Antidote:* Let the pastor bring his own organist or conduct the service with a printed order of service and hymns, if it is conducted from the funeral parlor.)

10. Organizing the service and everybody in it, and not enough attention to the pastor's requests because he is too busy directing. (*Antidote:* Let pastor and funeral director be in consultation so that each knows what the other is doing.)

Questions Pastors And Funeral Directors Can Ask Themselves

In order to examine these problems that exist between *some* pastors and *some* funeral directors, the following questions can be asked, in terms of a self-study and evaluation of the relationship, with a view to improving the relationship.

1. How well do I know him? Have I bothered to find out what he thinks?
2. Have I ever been with him socially? Would I enjoy knowing him on a social basis?
3. When was the last time I just sat and chatted with him, played

golf with him, served on a community project with him? In what have we really been interested to forge a common bond? Am I content just to engage in superficial pleasantries?

4. What are the roadblocks to communication as I see them?
5. What are the legitimate complaints I have to make? Can I put into writing my pet peeves?
6. Have I gone out of my way to let him know that what he did— the way he handled that family situation—pleased me? When I noticed a family not reacting, what did we do about it?
7. What are the things that could improve the service I render? Did I feel I did the best possible job with the grief sufferer(s)?
8. Did we work cooperatively, as possible team members, supporting each other?

Positive Factors Which Affect Rapport

Rapport is a perfectly good word meaning a harmonious relationship. Did we or did we not hit it off with each other? If communication does take place and dialogue begins to happen, these factors, among others, will have a positive bearing on whether rapport is achieved:

1. Warm, friendly, receptive attitudes.
2. Unhurried and unharried communication.
3. Genuine understanding of and respect for the other person as a person.
4. Acceptance of the other person and his operational set of givens.
5. Permissive atmosphere in which both listen to what is being said and reflect upon what the other is saying.
6. Responsible self-direction.
7. Ability to sustain positive attitudes under upsetting routines and circumstances.
8. Emotional, mental, moral health.
9. Personal integrity.

New possibilities present themselves when factors like the above are considered forthrightly, with candor. For the most part, pastors and funeral directors have worked side-by-side, in a not too glamorous undertaking. It was discovered, in the depth interviews reported in Chapter Nine, that there was very little to criticize, because both have drunk deeply at the well of the experiences of life and entered into a meaningful relationship, and because they are emotionally secure in themselves. They are providing a meaningful service, getting beyond such issues as open and closed caskets, where the service is to be held, and the price attached to the service.

The best relationships between pastors and funeral directors are those in which personal friendships have developed through the years and there is a mutual respect for each other as persons. Where the funeral director is a member of the parish, another kind of deepening relationship exists. Where pastors and funeral directors work most closely in a cooperative way, influence can be exerted in mutually helpful ways. What the pastor thinks will be communicated to other funeral directors and will be translated into the relationship that ultimately affects the persons being served—the grief sufferers.

Negative Factors Observed About Some Clergy By Funeral Directors

1. Pomposity and position consciousness.
2. Stereotyped behavior, as well as things said over and over again without much effect or meaning.
3. Throwing their weight around with families.
4. Lack of consideration of feelings of others.
5. "Going through the motions."
6. Hostility exhibited by cool aloofness from the whole business which they would just as soon finish in order to get back to more agreeable tasks.

Positive Factors Observed By Funeral Directors About Most Clergy

1. As a rule we find them cooperative and pleasant persons; there are always exceptions to every rule.
2. They provide meaningful services for the grief sufferer.
3. They are essentially men of integrity and good will.
4. They have poise in the presence of a seemingly hopeless situation.
5. They give comfort and reassurance to the living; this is the chief benefit that accrues from the service they render. It is a witness to faith in a crucial hour. We are grateful for every opportunity to assist the pastor because we are both trying to serve families who have asked us to do some very specific things. We do not usurp their function, nor would we ask them to do the things we have been called upon to do.

Buffalo Pilot Project

Germ-seed of an idea. The germ-seed of the idea grew out of the chance meeting on a panel of a pastor and a funeral director. They discussed other successful interfaith ventures that the pastor-chaplain had promoted in the local Council of Churches to help educate the pastors in the community and to foster better interpersonal and interprofessional relationships. Through consultation and cultivation of personal friendship over a period of two years, the project was finally launched in October of 1961.

Mechanics of the program. The Chaplains Department of the local Council of Churches of Buffalo and Erie County and the Erie-Niagara Funeral Directors Association were the co-sponsors of the project. The idea was to invite a distinguished speaker to address the group of pastors and funeral directors attending the area meeting at the University of Buffalo School of Medicine. Originally, it was projected on an interfaith basis; however, Roman Catholic clergy did not participate, although Roman Catholic funeral directors did. There were also a number of Jewish funeral directors and rabbis present.

Invitations were mailed with return postcards to predetermine the size of the group. A flyer was sent out to clergy through the Council of Churches. The local funeral directors circularized their own constituency. Area telephone committees were set up, and funeral directors personally called the clergy in their areas to invite them to the meeting. Transportation was provided for those who desired it. At first it was thought that this should be an all-day affair with opportunity to engage in fruitful conversation in buzz sessions with resource leaders, but it was finally decided that it be an evening meeting with an outstanding mental health authority as the featured attraction. It was projected at this time that this was not to be the only gathering of its kind, but that it would be followed up with neighborhood meetings.

Registration was handled by the funeral directors, and publicity was covered jointly by a public relations consultant employed by the funeral directors and the Council of Churches. Good press coverage was afforded. A number of the members of the medical community were also invited.

The theme of the conference. The theme of the conference was: "Grief Work—the Funeral and Mental Health." The principal speaker was Dr. Clemens E. Benda, director of the Fernald School, Waltham, Massachusetts, psychiatrist at Massachusetts General Hospital, recognized authority on *"grief work,"* and long-time associate of Dr. Erich Lindemann, chief of Harvard University department of psychiatry. Together they worked with the victims and families of the Boston Cocoanut Grove fire, and since then have had a continuing interest in the process of grief as it relates to those interested within the "caretaking group"—principally clergy and funeral directors.

The actual address by Dr. Benda was entitled: "Grief Work with the Bereaved in Its Application for the Ministry and the Funeral Director."[5]

Out of the four hundred invited, more than three hundred clergy and funeral directors heard Dr. Benda outline the essential characteristics of the grief process from the psychiatric point of view. Dr. Benda asserted that the sympathetic friend who tries to patch over his friend's grief in the death of a loved one may be doing more harm than good. According to his definition: "Grief work is an active effort on the part of the bereaved to realize and incorporate the image of the loss which he has suffered."

Funeral rites, the clergy, funeral directors, as well as doctors and nurses all play a part in working out grief through healthy psychological channels. No attempt should be made to deny legitimate emotions of grief to the bereaved. Dr. Benda went on to say: "We must all develop respect for letting people express their emotions. Holding back emotions and taking sedatives or tranquilizers can be harmful and only delay necessary grief reaction." He said that there is no easy way, and he urged ministers to expect bereaved persons to show strong feelings of guilt and hostility. Ministers should not be affected

---

[5] Subsequently published as *"Bereavement and Grief Work"* in the *Journal of Pastoral Care,* Spring, 1962.

by these reactions, but should listen patiently. Meeting friends at the funeral home, viewing the body, and attending the funeral may help the bereaved accept the fact that the loved one is gone forever.

After the presentation of the paper there was ample time allotted for questions. During the question and answer period the moderator (the writer) fielded the questions, printed on 3" × 5" cards, that were sent up to the platform. The many questions could not be answered from the floor, so they were all typed and prepared as thought primers for the follow-up meetings when the clergy and funeral directors would gather in the ensuing months to engage in dialogue and face-to-face relationship, and to discuss these mutual concerns, problems, and the kind of communication that should exist between them. This was projected as a follow-up, learning situation, concerning the psychology of grief as it applied to the people they are to serve mutually.

Recordings were made of the entire proceedings in case other area groups of funeral directors and clergy wanted to understand what took place at Buffalo and to learn from that experience if it could be applied in their area.

Inquiries were received from other areas. The experience at the Buffalo Pilot Project helped the Allegheny (Pennsylvania) County clergy and funeral directors to stage a successful interfaith program along the lines suggested above.

All who attended received packets of literature, which included the following material: "The Therapy of Grief," by William Clyde Donald; "The Funeral an Experience of Value," by Dr. Paul Irion; the *Good Housekeeping* article of April 1960 on "The Hurt That Heals," and Dr. Edgar Jackson's article, "The Role of the Funeral in the Grief Situation."

Subsequently, four or five neighborhood and denominational meetings were held where panel discussion, seminars, and papers were presented for mutual discussion. When the funeral directors met with the clergy in these neighborhood or denominational meetings, the tensions and confusions that existed were brought out into the open, talked about, and dissipated.

One denominational group was all ready to issue a "white paper," in the form of an ultimatum to the Funeral Directors Association, about what they expected and what they will and will not do. When the group finally met, such rapport was developed that they forgot all about the issuance of such a "decree." They are now trying, in their own way, to examine the life of their own parish to discover ways in which to provide meaningful services for each individual grief sufferer. The most heartening thing is that they were trying to meet human need at the level on which it is, not where they would like for it to be—all neatly packaged.

Where these area meetings have been held, both funeral directors and pastors are beginning to notice that they have much more to say to each other and to contribute to each other. At least the dialogue has begun.[6]

Cultivation of friendship, engaging in sports activities, serving on committees together, as well as area meetings, and mutual support will result in better funeral practice and better pastoral care, because a climate of understanding will be created for the kind of communication and cooperative venture both seek. The community will be better for creating the proper kind of atmosphere for those who mourn. A service will be provided that cannot be measured in dollars and cents but is measured in the lives and souls of people.

---

[6] It has been reported that since these original words were written in May, 1963, an estimated 7500 clergy, as well as funeral directors, have been involved in area meetings since the Buffalo Pilot Project in October of 1961.

CHAPTER NINE

CURRENT PARISH PATTERNS
And PRACTICES

It is difficult to be objective about death. The pastor is no more immune to subjective reaction to death and grief than is his parishioner. Both are potential grief sufferers; both are potential statistics in objective studies.

In order to gain an overview of current parish patterns and practices, a questionnaire study was conducted among 1000 pastors:

	Sent	Returned
The Lutheran Church in America (*Synod of New York*)	340	185
The Council of Churches of Buffalo and Erie County	376	164
The Methodist Church (*Genesee Conference*)	129	58
Chaplain Supervisors of The Institute of Pastoral Care	68	31
Niagara County Council of Churches	54	24
The Episcopal Church (*Diocese of Western N.Y.*)	33	10
	1000	472

The majority of the pastors were selected from the writer's own denomination in the State of New York, in which Synod he holds membership, and from the local Council of Churches in Buffalo, of which he is Director of the Chaplains Department. An attempt was made to include larger segments of Methodists and Episcopalians in addition to those who are members of the Councils of Churches. The chaplain supervisors of The Institute of Pastoral Care were included to give wider distribution nationally among a group of well-trained, clinically oriented pastors. It was felt that this would provide some basis of comparison to the state and local picture. It was also the feeling of the writer that knowing about his own denomination, the Council constituency that he serves, and the supervisors to whom he is related directly might give a much better picture than random sampling in a wider distribution on a national basis. This may account, in part, for the larger percentage of returns than is ordinarily expected in questionnaire studies.

In addition to the survey, depth interviews were held with twelve local parish pastors. The same general areas were covered as were represented in the survey.

While the questionnaire was designed to give some objective data, it became evident as the returned questionnaires were evaluated that subjective reaction was quite marked. The covering letter suggested that the "questionnaire is designed to be provocative and stimulating. You may want to write more than is asked. If you should desire to enlarge your answers, please use the reverse side of the questionnaire." Strong feelings were elicited. More than 25 percent wrote marginal notes and comments; some wrote two-page letters. In other returns the entire backs of the papers were filled with handwritten or typed comments. This was especially true of Question 18, which asked for "pet gripes."

In reporting the questionnaire study, some interpretive remarks will follow the tabulated results. In conjunction with the question being raised, evaluation of the depth interviews has been added, where pertinent. The reader may wish to register his own response separately and compare his answer with those of the respondents.

1. WHAT IS YOUR VIEW OF DEATH? (Rank in the order of importance a, b, c, etc.)

First choices

a. Fear it	24
b. Haven't thought much about it	37

c. Feel it is a long way off   46
d. Looking forward to it   62
e. Regret leaving tasks undone   152
f. Other   147

The subjective nature of this response is one of the evidences cited for the statement that it is difficult to be objective toward one's own death. In his own reaction the pastor expresses genuine regret when he realizes that he will be leaving tasks undone. He says he is looking forward to this phase of existence. In the category "Other," he indicates concern for what will be happening to his family, as well as avowing the Christian hope of an eternal existence. This ambivalence is represented in the pastors' responses.

Depth Interview Question: What Is Your Reaction to Death (Your Own)?

The predominant theme, running through the depth interviews, is the regret of leaving tasks undone. While there is no feeling of fear, there is the sense of facing the unknown. They express the possibility of nonfulfillment. "I want to see a bit more of the game through. . . ." "Death would be a burden because opportunities would be cut off." "Often death is thought of as a friend, especially among the aged, a tyrant robbing of life among the young. At different stages of development death may seem far off, something to fear, something that hurts those who survive, and there is a need to grow toward acceptance of the fact. . . ." "Death is a complete break with the life I have known and becomes a dramatic transition into an existence which is difficult to describe . . . the human vocabulary is not adequate for such a radical transition."

2. Have You Had a Loss in Your Family Within the Last Two Years?

Yes   170

No   302

Most everything that the pastors report will be colored more by this one factor than any other. While death may be seen objectively when it is happening to another's family, when it happens in the immediate family, many feelings and memories are aroused.

Depth Interviews:

When this question was asked, only two of the pastors interviewed had had a loss within the prescribed period. Their answers were conditioned in the light of it. One seemed to have accepted the fact and it had become a basic criterion of his existence. He knew that his parents were going to die very soon and he said he prepared himself for it. For the other pastor whose father died after a lingering illness, death was viewed as welcome "because it is more than you can take to see a person reduced and degraded."

3. What Is Your Attitude Toward Grief? Grief Is—(Please rank)

First choices

a. A healthy emotional response	150
b. A necessary emotional outlet	114
c. Necessary but not essential for healthy adjustment	27
d. Don't feel everybody should go through this experience	9
e. Other	23

It appears that the clustering about the two first choices indicates that grief is understood as a normal process and is essentially a necessary part of the appropriate reaction to pain of loss. This is interpreted to mean loss in significant relationships and it is undoubtedly limited to loss through death. No one seemed to indicate that grief is a response to other significant kinds of loss mentioned heretofore.

Depth Interviews:

All pastors interviewed felt that grief is an essential ingredient in the healing process and recovery of equilibrium. Whereas, at one time they would have tended to cover up the overt emotional response, they now feel that this must be encouraged. The pastor's role, it was felt, is to "help them express it." In the views of these pastors it was found that grief is a "normal kind of outlet for intense feeling. . . ." "It has to be accepted, faced, and worked through." Two of the pastors felt it difficult to express grief themselves. One had been through two recent losses and the other was having difficulty with an unresolved grief reaction that had persisted for a period of six years. Grief, as one of them recounted, "is a real part of a person's need to deal with loss. You can't cut this thing off because there is going to be deep hurt."

4. HAVE YOU OBSERVED UNUSUAL GRIEF REACTIONS?

a. Sufferer becoming depressed?	418
b. Sufferer becoming elated?	100
c. Sufferer dropping out of Church?	276
d. Sufferer becoming bitter toward God?	416
e. Quick marriage after death?	224

It is interesting to note that the psychological (a) and theological (d) responses are more frequently made—the one, an outward manifestation of the inner, unexpressed feeling. All responses appear with enough regularity to indicate that the pastor should be alert to possible danger signals in the grief sufferers within his parish.

Depth Interviews:

The pastors in this phase of the study were asked the same question in a slightly different form: *What are the basic problems you have encountered in the helping process with the grief sufferer?* The responses indicated the gamut of expression outlined above. In addition, there were such factors as: (1) loss of purpose; (2) withdrawal into an emotional jungle; (3) lack of continuity; (4) castigation of self for lack of faith and guilt feelings; (5) nonacceptance of reality as well as an attempt to escape; (6) nervousness and sleeplessness; (7) alcoholism. They noted that marriage too soon after death has revitalized the old partner, "marrying an idolized image of the partner who died . . . then expecting fulfillment and happy

5. IN YOUR GRIEF WORK WITH PARISHIONERS DO YOU: (Please rank)

	First choices
a. Encourage talk about deceased?	219
b. Review the past events?	28
c. Talk about funeral arrangements?	51
d. Try to discourage any talk about deceased?	3
e. Find it difficult to get survivors to talk about deceased?	2
f. Get bereaved busy doing useful things?	53
g. Other	21

marriage and not finding fulfillment or happiness." There are some who are the "brittle type; if they let go, they would break."

In evaluating this question it is important to realize that the pastor usually works *a*, followed by *b* (130 ranked second), and then *c* (95 ranked third). Getting the "bereaved busy doing useful things" seems to follow the logical order, as the fourth choice. The latter may not be the most therapeutic thing, if this is attempted too soon or without too much consideration. Just to be doing things is not a substitute for deliberating and planning action before it is initiated.

Depth Interviews:

The question was asked in slightly different form: *What do you feel is a healthy reaction to grief?* The responses were expressed in terms of encouraging the grief sufferer to cry because it has a therapeutic effect. "Sometimes," said one pastor, "you have to help it along; it's like lancing a boil. . . ." "Keeping it bottled up is not going to do any good; you have to get it out and thus put it in proper perspective. . . ." "One must express it in appropriate ways, talking about the deceased, doing practical things, accepting the fact that no relationship is perfect and facing it honestly . . . grief in proportion to the loss." One pastor was quite insistent that "more problems are encountered with people who arrange memorial services and shut themselves off from friends."

6. WHAT RESOURCES HAVE YOU FOUND MOST USEFUL IN WORKING WITH THE GRIEF SUFFERER? (Please rank)

		First choices
a.	Scripture	57
b.	Prayer	113
c.	Listening	263
d.	Short-term counseling	19
e.	Long-term counseling	5
f.	Other factors	4

It is readily noted that the pastor thinks listening and prayer are most helpful in ministering to the grief sufferer. Since very few are following the grief sufferer with any short-term counseling, the pastor may be missing opportunities to render more definitive service in his post-funeral calls. There seems also to be a correlation between this Question and Question 10. There is a relatively insignificant number being seen in a counseling relationship as a result of grief suffering.

Depth Interviews:

Two questions attempted to get at similar feelings in the pastors interviewed. *How do you counsel people—do you give sermons about the grief process? If you preached a sermon on grief, what would you say by way of outline?* Most of the pastors have done little by way of sermons other than introducing the matter of grief in Lenten messages. One pastor felt that "people don't really want to talk about this." It can be tied up with the teaching life of the church in meaningful ways. Several of the pastors have held seminars on grief and death and the funeral. One stated, "It is difficult to give something of the eternal to the people who are dealing in earthly issues." Most do not attempt any kind of explanation in counseling. The work with the grief sufferers, in the particular situations they encounter, generally follows the procedural steps in Question 5.

What do you feel are the unique resources of the Church in dealing with the grief sufferer? This question elicited some philosophical principles as well as some practical aids. The responses were phrased in the following ways: "Eternal life is a thing that is held up. It would be considered tragic if there were no hope . . . The Gospel deals with both life and death and has a word . . . This is the meaning of the Christian faith. God goes through it with us. When standing by the grief sufferer, you can't explain what it means, you personify the Presence of Christ . . ." "The pastor has something to talk about besides (the man's) qualifications . . . People have access to me as pastor and help is mediated more through personality . . . theological abstractions are not very comforting . . ." "The Church offers a philosophy of life, a source of strength and assurance of this continuity . . ." "The Church becomes a relay station . . . it offers a community of concerned people . . . Through the pastor the Church offers the possibility of talking through the grief . . . There is the deep concern of the fellowship of Christians."

There seems to be no significant difference in either the pastors interviewed or the survey respondents with regard to this procedure. The general feeling is that the pastor goes as soon as he knows or hears. "If I am close, I would be called . . ." "Too often the call

7. WHAT DO YOU DO WHEN YOU HEAR ABOUT THE DEATH OF A MEMBER? (Please rank)

	First choices
a. Go to the home right away	396
b. Wait to be called by family	23
c. Wait to be called by funeral director	9
d. Other	11

comes from the funeral director, after the funeral preparations are made and the announcement is already on the way to the newspaper." This latter response is one of the most prevalent complaints or gripes of pastors (indicated in Question 18) as a source of discomfiture. The conclusion to be drawn is that the pastor should be available to the grief sufferer under all circumstances. It should make no real difference from what source he may be called to be of service.

8. DO YOU MAKE PRE-FUNERAL CALLS TO THE HOME AFTER YOU ARE NOTIFIED OF THE DEATH?

a. Always	391
b. Occasionally	52
c. Not usually	7
d. No	0
(No answer	22)

9. DO YOU FOLLOW UP WITH CALLS IN THE HOME?

a. Always	320
b. Occasionally	104
c. Not usually	3
d. No	0
(No answer	45)

The responses to these two questions are seen as expectations of the parishioner. They are really a continuation of the line of approach used in Question 7. When the deceased is not a member of the Church, the pastor will usually go to the funeral home to meet with the family. It would be a rare occasion that would prevent the pastor from seeing the family before the funeral, even when there is no connection with the pastor's specific congregation. Funeral directors report in a separate survey, however, that pastors do not always make the most of this opportunity.

The majority of respondents who made marginal notes indicate that the post-funeral call is the most important aspect of the work they do with the grief sufferer.

10. How Many People Are You Currently Seeing in Counseling Concerning a Problem of Grief?

Average

a. As a result of death   2
b. As a result of some other form of grief crisis, such as separation, divorce, etc.   2

A total of 839 grief sufferers, through loss by death, are being seen by the 472 pastors in this study. While a considerable number of pastors are seeing none, the range is from 0 to 30. The same respondents are seeing 1099 parishioners in other grief crises and the range is from 0 to 40. Neither long-term nor short-term counseling with the grief sufferer is being done by very many pastors. This indicates, therefore, that many grief sufferers are not being counseled over any protracted period. Post-funeral calls seem to be the only follow-up contact. One mental hospital chaplain indicated that the majority of the people he sees in his daily ministry are in the mental hospital because of some unresolved grief reaction. He reports this not because he is looking for this as a part of the syndrome of mental illness.

Questions 11 through 15 must be studied as a whole in order for

11. Do You Favor Church Funerals?

Yes   406
No   33
(No answer   33)

12. Do You Conduct Most of Your Funerals From the Funeral Home or From the Church?

Funeral home   406
Church   41
Makes no difference   25

the inner correlation of the findings to become apparent. We will give them with the resultant tabulations and then make the interpretative remarks of the questions as a whole.

13. Do You Favor Memorial Services?

Yes	250
No	147
(Undecided	75)

14. In Your Area Is There a Trend Toward Memorial Services?

Yes	76
No	347
(No answer	49)

15. Do You Feel the Funeral Serves a vital Function in the Grief Process?

Yes	407
No	43
(No answer	22)

It is interesting to note that the same number of respondents who favor the church funeral conduct their funerals almost exclusively from the funeral home. The fact that most of the funerals are conducted from the funeral home and not from the Church is attributed to the following factors noted by both the survey respondents and the pastors in the depth interviews: (1) The pastors have not educated their people regarding their personal preference. (2) The funeral directors have done a pretty good job of promoting the funeral from their establishments and are often maligned as favoring this because it gives them opportunity "to show off their work." Most funeral directors known to the writer are happy to cooperate with the pastor in his requests, if the family requests the church funeral, and there is no difference in the cost, as is often maintained. (3) There may be some psychological handicaps in conducting the funeral from the Church. While it is felt that the Christian ought to be buried from the Church and that this is the natural ending of a cycle which began with baptism, the grief sufferer may be unable to stand the pain that this memory may arouse when he attempts to go back to worship in the Church. Holding the funeral in the funeral home permits a much greater degree of freedom to accept the ministrations of the Church. Too often in the cultural setting of the traditional American funeral (except in many small towns and rural areas where there are many Sunday funerals) the community of the concerned—the Church— rarely rallies about the deceased unless he is some prominent figure. Many are unable or unwilling to forego a day's pay to attend a funeral. The size of the funeral, therefore, is small and there is something psychologically empty about holding a funeral in a large sanctuary with only a few friends and relatives attending.

The majority of those respondents who favor the memorial service also feel that the funeral serves a vital function in the grief process. This appears to be a contradiction or a misunderstanding of the term memorial service, which usually means a service held in the Church without the presence of the body. The committal is conducted as a private affair, or the body may have been cremated before the service. This seems to meet a real need on the part of some, including the pastor, to mask the reality of death as something unreal. The spiriting away of the body and the gathering of the remnant afterwards does not, as has been indicated, accord with the desire of most men to be remembered and not so carelessly shunted aside.

In considering those who favor the memorial service there are only 22 more than the combined group of those who do not favor the memorial service and those with qualified answers or no answers. The *yes* in many cases is a qualified one. "Yes, though I seldom conduct one." "I have never conducted one." "Yes, I would like it for the entire Church." "Yes, in circumstances where necessary grief work may be done."

It was noted in the depth interviews that "the ceremonial funeral" is preferred by the pastors interviewed. "The service ought to have a connection with the body." "It is only those who have had a close connection with the church who are usually buried from the Church."

There is no significant trend toward the memorial service in any area. The majority of respondents are from the metropolitan areas and towns under 10,000 population. Most of the memorial services are held in the larger metropolitan areas. The memorial service is another evidence of depersonalization in American culture.

16. How Many Funerals Do You Conduct on an Average During a Year?

One to ten	186
Ten to twenty	189
Twenty to thirty	40
Thirty to forty	21
Over forty	18

17. How Many Different Funeral Directors Do You Work with During the Course of a Year?

One to five	336
Five to ten	100
Ten to fifteen	8
Over fifteen	6

The majority of pastors conduct from one to twenty funerals per year. This would mean an average of approximately one funeral per month. They are acquainted and work with from one to five funeral directors. The following question is the most telling with regard to the relationship of the funeral director and the pastor.

18. Assuming There Is a Need to Improve Relationships with Funeral Directors, How Do You Feel They Can Be Improved? (Please rank)

	First choices
a. Through closer cooperation	118
b. Through better understanding between each profession	240
c. Through neighborhood meetings	34
d. Through social contacts	11
e. Other	30

(The questionnaire asked for pet gripes.)

The strong opinions stated in connection with this question indicate that there is not only a need to improve relationships with funeral directors but also a constructive way in which this can be accomplished. The pet gripes reported in Chapter Eight indicate that there is enough smoke to spell *fire*. The realization on the part of the pastors that there is something missing in their relationships with funeral directors indicates that pastors are as troubled by it as are the funeral directors. The cultivation of pastoral relationships by funeral directors has become a national preoccupation. The two professions need to know each other better. Knowing how to talk to one another will relieve the confusion and tension. There are not large numbers of pastors who feel that the funeral director is *money mad* or an unscrupulous businessman. The pet gripes are limited to those who have had bad experiences with some funeral directors. This represents 20 percent of the respondents. Many funeral directors consider this an alarming proportion and are making every effort to promote meetings along the lines of the Buffalo Pilot Project.

19. Do You Feel Area Meetings of the Clergy and Funeral Directors Are a Means of Reaching Better Understanding?

a. I favor it	307
b. I do not favor it	69
c. I would attend such a meeting on a neighborhood basis	240
(No answer	20)

This question seems to confirm that there is a favorable climate for promoting pastor-funeral director relationships. While neighborhood meetings have not been tried to any great extent, perhaps area meetings may be the answer to better understanding and cooperation.

20. How Well Do You Know the Funeral Director in Your Neighborhood?

a. Have gone by to get acquainted	132
b. He has come by to get acquainted with me	89
c. We never see each other except at funerals	187
d. Have been socially connected with funeral directors	145
e. Other	140

This response confirms the writer's contention regarding the necessity of mutual understanding of each profession, if the grief sufferer is to benefit. While the majority of respondents indicate that they did not see much of the funeral director except in the official performance of the duties, the combined totals of *d* and *e* seem to indicate that there is more socialization going on than was suspected. There is a genuine regard for each other, and the vast majority of pastors (approximately 75 percent) indicate that they do not experience any difficulty with the funeral directors with whom they are acquainted and work during the course of the year.

21. WHICH OF THE FOLLOWING BOOKS HAVE YOU READ IN THE FIELD?

And Peace at the Last, Russell Dicks & Thomas S. Kepler	57
The American Funeral, Leroy Bowman	50
The Funeral, Andrew Blackwood	190
The Funeral And The Mourners, Paul Irion	80
Understanding Grief, Edgar Jackson	187
Ye Shall Be Comforted, William Rogers	111
Others	139
(None	139)

Andrew Blackwood wrote about the funeral long before the modern emphasis on grief psychology and he concentrated more on the conduct of the funeral than on the reaction of the grief sufferer. More recently the work of Edgar Jackson has gained wider readership. Since the writer has personal acquaintance with these authors, he would not run the risk of putting them in any sequential order. With the execption of *The American Funeral*, by Bowman, he could unhesitatingly commend all of the other books listed in this question. Bowman may be read to get a point of view that opposes the modern grief psychology which the other authors represent.

Noteworthy is the fact that almost a third of the respondents have not read any of these most recent writings. Among "Others" that have been listed, two monographs for the layman, expressing the meaning of grief—*Good Grief*, by Granger Westberg and *You and Your Grief*, by Edgar Jackson—have been widely used as books that could be given to the grief sufferer for reading in the weeks after the funeral. Those who have tried to give them during the initial stages of the grief reaction have found that they were less meaningful than after a short time had elapsed. It is the conviction of the writer that there is no substitute for the personal one-to-one relationships with the grief sufferer. Books are important to the extent that they are guidelines and furnish additional information and ways of looking at things, but the greater value is derived from the encounter of pastor and grief sufferer.

Who is this pastor we have been analyzing and what makes him react to grief in the way he does? He is a composite drawn from many facets of ministerial life. At the end of the questionnaire we tried to have the respondent tell us something about himself. The pastor whom we have been asking about his current parish practices is between thirty-five and forty-five years of age, is serving a congregation with approximately 500 members, and has been in his parish from one to five years. His church is located in a larger metropolitan area. He has little or no clinical pastoral training.

The pastor is on the "front line" of the experience of the grief sufferer. In time of grief crisis he is there standing by the sufferer in his distress. The writer hopes that this volume will offer some encouragement to the pastor to improve his counseling skills and to gain competency in rendering a more adequate ministry to the grief sufferer.

APPENDIX

NOTEWRITING OUTLINE FOR VERBATIM INTERVIEWS

*CCB, 63, I, 1
1/1/63

Supervisor's Comments

A 3½-inch margin is allowed on the left-hand side of the page, a one inch on the right.

Never use name or initials of patients. One suggested system of identifying symbols is: CCB (Pastor's initials), 63 (year), I (Identifies the parishioner), 1 (Identifies the page). *

Give thoughtful attention to these introductory items and be sure nothing is omitted. #

First Visit

Write here what factual information you have learned about patient *prior* to visit, that is, male, age 42, painter, single, Baptist, admitted 1/1/63 with diagnosis of gastric ulcer.

After first visit omit this section.

Incorporate new information under "preliminary plans."

#Preliminary Plans: Use (1) for a first visit; use (2) only for later visits.

(1) For a first visit:

Knowing what you do about the patient, prepare your mind for the visit. Imagine the situation in which you may find yourself upon arrival. Describe how you can best introduce yourself. Make sure that you are going as one who wishes to make a friend.

In a sentence, describe this planning before making the visit.

— 2 — (number pages consecutively through the entire relationship.)

(2) For future visits:

List the things you *do not* wish to do. Then list the specific things you would like to have result from this visit—information, conversational subjects, attitudes, understanding, etc. This list should grow out of your preceding summary.

Be very sure not to carry the above with you as an agenda. Permit this planning to prepare your mind, not control your visit.

The Visit:

Use the first paragraph for your first impressions of patient, including description of physical facts about the patient, your introduction, his attitude toward you, his attitude in general.

Then give a general account of what took place, not only conversation but also little incidents, embarrassment, loss of conversation, etc. Preserve all transitions so the report will be a unified whole. (*Make* the report as *objective* as a good news account. Reserve all judgments and interpretations for the conclusion.)

% Conclusion: (in three parts)

(1) *Analyze* what took place. Be sure to offer interpretations of

For recording direct discourse indent as follows:

C: I am Pastor B., Protestant Chaplain here in the hospital.

P: I'm happy to meet you.

C: How are things going with you?

It has become clear that all three parts of this conclusion are of vital importance. A later call cannot be made with as much efficiency if any part of the conclusion is neglected. %

This type of conclusion can become a private laboratory which is second in importance only to the later enlarged laboratory of the seminar. It should be written soon after, if not immediately following, the visit. The written notes should be read and the entire visit reviewed with the points of this conclusion in mind before the actual conclusion is written.

any puzzling elements in the conversation, or indicate your inability to do so. *State insights you may have had, whether confirmed or tentative,* which bear on material in notes.

Analyze your notes from the standpoint of association of subject matter. Indicate any items which because of repetition or relationship seem to have meaning.

(2) *Criticize* your part in visit. Note things that dissatisfied you, that you would rather have done in a different way. Mention successful elements pertaining to method which is worthy of further study and perhaps repetition in future work.

(3) State what you think to be the *task of the minister* in this case, both the long-range task and the immediate one. Thought should be given to this at the end of each visit.

Note *length of visit*—ten minutes or thirty minutes, etc.

For recording of Summary Accounts, the only difference is that the recording is done in paragraph form and is given in narrative fashion.

BIBLIOGRAPHY

BACHMANN, C. CHARLES, *The Development of Lutheran Pastoral Care in America*. Unpublished Doctoral dissertation, Boston University, 1949.

BLACKWOOD, ANDREW, *The Funeral*. Philadelphia: Westminister Press, 1942.

BOWMAN, LEROY, *The American Funeral*. Washington, D.C., Public Affairs Press, 1959.

CLERK, N. W., *A Grief Observed*. London: Faber and Faber, 1961.

DICKS, RUSSELL L., *The Art of Ministering to the Sick*. New York: Macmillan, 1936.

—— and THOMAS S. KEPLER, *And Peace at the Last*. Philadelphia: Westminster Press, 1953.

FARBEROW, NORMAN L. and EDWIN S. SHNEIDMAN, *The Cry for Help*. New York: McGraw-Hill, Inc., 1961.

GURIN, GERALD, JOSEPH VEROFF, and SHEILA FELD, *Americans View Their Mental Health*. New York: Basic Books Inc., 1960.

HABENSTEIN, ROBERT W. and WILLIAM M. LAMERS, *The History of American Funeral Directing*. Milwaukee: Bulfin Printers, Inc., 1955.

——, *Funeral Customs the World Over*. Milwaukee: Bulfin Printers, Inc., 1960.

HOWE, REUEL L., *The Miracle of Dialogue*. Greenwich: The Seabury Press, Inc., 1963.

IRION, PAUL E., *The Funeral and the Mourners*. New York: Abingdon Press, 1954.

JACKSON, EDGAR N., *Understanding Grief*. New York: Abingdon Press, 1957.

——, *You and Your Grief*. Great Neck, N.Y.: Channel Press Inc., 1961.

JOHNSON, PAUL E., *Psychology of Pastoral Care*. New York: Abingdon Press, 1953.

LEE, HARPER, *To Kill a Mockingbird*. Philadelphia: J. B. Lippincott Company, 1960.

LIEBMAN, JOSHUA L., *Peace of Mind*. New York: Simon & Schuster, 1946.

MARSHALL, CATHERINE, *To Live Again*. New York: McGraw-Hill, Inc., 1957.

ROGERS, CARL R., *Counseling and Psychotherapy*. Boston: Houghton Mifflin Co., 1942.

——, *Client-Centered Therapy*. Boston: Houghton Mifflin Co., 1951.

ROGERS, WILLIAM F., *The Place of Grief Work in Mental Health*. Unpublished Doctoral dissertation, Boston University, 1949.

——, *Ye Shall Be Comforted*. Philadelphia: Westminster Press, 1950.

TOURNIER, PAUL, *The Meaning of Persons*. New York: Harper & Row, Publisher, 1957.

WESTBERG, GRANGER E., *Minister and Doctor Meet*. New York: Harper and Row, Publisher, 1961.

——, *Good Grief*. Rock Island, Ill.: Augustana Press, 1962.

Other Publications

BENDA, CLEMENS E., "Bereavement and Grief Work," *Journal of Pastoral Care*, XVI, No. 1 (Spring 1962), 1–13.

DONALD, WILLIAM CLYDE, II, "The Therapy of Grief," in *History of the Michigan Funeral Directors Association*. Lansing, 1960.

ENGEL, GEORGE L., "Is Grief a Disease?" *Psychosomatic Medicine*, Vol. XXIII, No. 1 (January-February, 1961).

FREUD, SIGMUND, "Mourning and Melancholia," from *Collected Papers*, IV. London: Hogarth Press and The Institute of Psycho-Analysis, 1948.

FULTON, ROBERT L., "Attitudes of Clergymen Toward Funerals and Funeral Directors in the United States," St. Louis: National Funeral Directors Association of the United States, Inc., 1959.

——, "The Sacred and the Secular," St. Louis: National Funeral Directors Association of the United States, Inc., 1963.

IRION, PAUL E., "The Funeral: An Experience of Value." Address given at 75th Annual Convention of National Funeral Directors Association Meeting, Milwaukee, Wisconsin, 1956.

——— (guest editor), "The Funeral, Death, and Bereavement." *Pastoral Psychology,* June 1963.

KRUPP, GEORGE R. and BERNARD KLIGFELD, "The Bereavement Reaction: A Cross-cultural Evaluation." *Journal of Religion and Health,* published by The Academy of Religion and Mental Health, Vol. 1, No. 3 (April 1962).

LINDEMANN, ERICH, "Symptomatology and Management of Acute Grief," *American Journal of Psychiatry,* 101 (September 1944), 141, Reprinted in *Journal of Pastoral Care,* 5 (Fall 1951), 19–31.

———, "Psychological Aspects of Mourning," *The Director,* January 1961, 14–17. (An address delivered at National Funeral Directors Association Meeting, Denver, Colorado, 1960.)

INDEX